The Origins of Language

'This short guide to modern empirical research on language evolution provides a breezy and readable introduction to the many issues involved in understanding how humans came to possess one of our most prized capacities: our ability to acquire and use language.'

Tecumseh Fitch, University of Vienna

'Jim Hurford has produced a work of stunning depth and breadth, expertly condensed in this slim guide. These are notoriously difficult questions: How did the capacity for language evolve in the deep history of our species? How do different languages evolve in the more recent histories of our societies? Hurford is one of the few scholars with the authority and interdisciplinary reach to give us compelling and plausible answers. *The Origins of Language* is a rare achievement, and highly recommended.'

N. J. Enfield, Max Planck Institute, Nijmegen, and University of Sydney

'Hurford has written a delightful little book, an ideal point of entry into the range of complex issues facing anyone that wants to understand how human language evolved. Darwin himself would have cherished this guide.'

Cedric Boeckx, ICREA/Universitat de Barcelona

'No one has thought more deeply about the evolution of the human language faculty than James Hurford, and no one writes about the topic more engagingly. In this book he explains and synthesizes the most important findings concerning language evolution from across a wide variety of scientific disciplines, including linguistics, biology, ethology, psychology, and cognitive science. His writing is always grounded in evidence-based argumentation, yet is informative and clear for the non-specialist reader. To introduce in such a short work all the major aspects of the evolution of language—from the beginnings of a special human type of communication to the emergence of sound systems, through meaning to symbolic words to sentence structure—is an impressive feat. To make it not only thorough but thoroughly readable is a real achievement. A lovely little book: great fun, cogent and scientifically solid.'

astle University

T0352693

James R. Hurford is Emeritus Professor at the University of Edinburgh, where he was previously Professor of General Linguistics from 1979 until his retirement in 2009. Over the last 25 years he has pioneered the rebirth of serious scientific interest in the origins and evolution of language. He co-founded with Chris Knight the biennial international conferences on the evolution of language (known as EVOLANG), with Simon Kirby the Language Evolution and Computation Research Unit at the University of Edinburgh, and with Kathleen Gibson the OUP series on language evolution. His previous publications include *The Origins of Meaning* (OUP 2007) and *The Origins of Grammar* (OUP 2011).

The Origins of Language

A SLIM GUIDE

James R. Hurford

OXFORD
UNIVERSITY PRESS

OXFORD
UNIVERSITY PRESS

Great Clarendon Street, Oxford, OX2 6DP,
United Kingdom

Oxford University Press is a department of the University of Oxford.
It furthers the University's objective of excellence in research, scholarship,
and education by publishing worldwide. Oxford is a registered trade mark of
Oxford University Press in the UK and in certain other countries

Published in the United States of America by Oxford University Press
198 Madison Avenue, New York, NY 10016, United States of America

British Library Cataloguing in Publication Data

Data available

Library of Congress Cataloging in Publication Data

Data available

ISBN 978-0-19-870188-0

For Rosie and Sue, and in Eve's memory.

This *Slim Guide* aims to be non-technical, readable, and short, while still conveying what is unique and special about language and its continuity with non-human life. It shows the tips of many icebergs, which can be explored by further detailed reading, suggestions for which are given at the end of the book.

Contents

1

The prehistory of a very special ape

In this chapter I make a flying start, compressing millions of years, from the first bipedal ape to the first *Homo sapiens*, into a few pages. Some of the history of our lineage is now well agreed, but many details are uncertain, debated, and open to revision by the next fossil discovery. In outline, the history goes from the split with the chimpanzee lineage about 7 million years ago, through Australopithecine apes, through two *Homo* species, *habilis* and *erectus*, to the emergence of our own species about 200,000 years ago. From the scant fossil remains, we know a little about our remote ancestors' sizes and shapes, and for the more recent ones even just a little about their ways of life. In the last few years, it has been possible even to infer, albeit speculatively, a little about their ways of communicating, as we shall see later in this book. Researchers sometimes suggest that *Homo erectus*, a tall, robust ape from about 1.5 million years ago, may have had a 'protolanguage', a meaningful learned vocabulary but no grammar—just 'words' strung together. We have no direct way of knowing whether this was the case, but recently acquired knowledge does tend to point in that direction. Noam Chomsky has dismissed all talk of language evolution as 'fairy stories'. There are no fairies in this book, nor any other imaginary entities. We will reason only from real brains, real genes, real vocal tracts, real acoustic patterns, real fossils, and real social interaction, in humans or other animals. Indeed, we can only speculate about how and why languages and the human capacity for language got to be the way they are. We can't travel back in time to observe, and there are no literal echoes of people speaking way back then. This applies to all speculation about the past, from the geological formation of the earth to what happened right after the Big Bang that made the universe. There are better and worse stories, in terms of internal coherence, economy, and consistency with available facts.

Researchers in language evolution try to collect as much relevant information as they can from genetics, child language development, neuroscience, palaeontology, anthropology, comparative psychology, linguistic typology, historical linguistics, and computer modelling to build as coherent a picture as possible of how and why languages and the unique human capacity for language evolved. The interdisciplinary nature of the quest is challenging and exciting in itself. I hope this book will persuade you that sensible things can be said about language origins and evolution. We will not be able to answer many 'When?' questions, such as when words or complex sentences were first used. To any 'Where?' question, the only, very vague answer is 'Somewhere in Africa'. Just as important are the 'How?' and 'Why?' questions. Considering these questions adds satisfyingly to our understanding of what language is. We will see language in the light of evolution—a perspective interestingly different from other views. Some knowledge of our prehistory after diverging from the other apes is useful as background, and I will now whizz through those seven million years, summarizing consensus views and noting what we can glean from the palaeontological record, relevant to the origins of language.

We humans are primates, a zoological order that includes the monkeys and apes. We are great apes, and most closely related to the chimpanzees and bonobos. Much research has found greater cognitive capacities in apes than in monkeys. Within the apes, lesser apes, e.g. gibbons, are distinguished from the great apes, the chimpanzees, bonobos, gorillas, and orang-utans. Chimpanzees and bonobos are evolutionarily close to each other; indeed, bonobos were only recently recognized as a separate species. The line leading to humans split off from that leading to bonobos and chimpanzees about 7 million years ago. It is usually assumed that there have been fewer changes in the bonobo/chimpanzee lineage than in ours.

So, with caution, we assume that our ancestors of 6 million years ago had something like the body shape, behaviour, and cognitive capacities of modern bonobos and chimpanzees. Bonobos may be a bit more like us cognitively than chimpanzees, but bonobo/chimpanzee differences are slight.

A prominent landmark in the human lineage was the advent of habitual bipedalism. The extant non-human apes sometimes walk upright on two feet. Bonobos even seem to do it with some ease, when they need to, as when they have their hands full, but it's not their normal mode of getting around. The *Australopithecus* (literally 'southern ape') genus, consisting of one or more species (nobody knows how many) was the first definitely habitual bipedal ape, living in eastern and southern Africa. The transition from occasional bipedalism to habitual bipedalism was not abrupt but gradual, like everything else in evolution. Given the long time periods involved, and the scarcity of specimens, transitions may seem abrupt. Australopithecines have been dated to a long period, between about 4 and 2 million years ago. The specimen known as Lucy was an Australopithecine, as was the so-called Taung child, and Australopithecines left their footprints in the volcanic ash at Laetoli, in what is now Tanzania. Our knowledge of Australopithecines is based on a small sample of partial skeletons, including about half a dozen more or less complete skulls, and some knee joints. Australopithecines walked on two feet, though probably not as upright as us, as can be inferred from the shapes of the pelvis and knee joints and the base of the skull (basicranium). This first bipedal gait started the process of freeing the rhythm of breathing from that of walking and running, a helpful step toward the production of speech, much later in evolution. Bipedalism also freed the hands for potential meaningful gestures. Australopithecines had brains no bigger than those of modern chimpanzees. No relics exist of tools made by them, but chimpanzees make tools, so probably Australopithecines did too, and they have not survived; only stones survive from so long ago, and as far as we know Australopithecines didn't make stone tools. They were sexually dimorphic, with males bigger than females, like modern gorillas, from which we can infer that their social and family arrangements were unlike ours. Even the males were small, less than 1.5 metres tall, and weighing only up to about 50 kilos. They appear to have had a vegetarian diet. Apart from the bipedalism, this genus has less in common with modern humans than with other modern apes; its significance is as our remote ancestor.

After the Australopithecines, *Homo habilis* 'clever man' is the species often (though not with great certainty) held to be next in the human lineage. *Habilis*, the first *Homo* species, lived in East Africa between about 2.5 and 1.5 million years ago. *Habilis* is so named because the species were the first to make stone tools, which were very crude, basically pebbles with enough knocked off to make a sharp edge. This tool industry is known as the Oldowan industry, after the Olduvai gorge in Tanzania where many specimens have been found. Oldowan tools are not complex enough to suggest any language-like skills. The very fact of making stone tools indicates patience, postponement of gratification, a mind capable of foresight into future needs, and constructive planning, qualities found only in limited ways in modern non-human apes.

Next in the story of our lineage is *Homo erectus* 'upright man', who were robust and as tall as well-nourished modern humans. There is debate over how *erectus* and (possibly) another species, *Homo ergaster*, are related. Both lived in Africa during the same period, between 1.8 million and 1 million years ago, and some of them are associated with a more advanced stone technology, the Acheulian industry. Making Acheulian tools demands much more time, patience, and foresight than the Oldowan technology, indicating a mental advance over *Homo habilis*. Starting in Africa, some groups of *erectus* migrated out to Europe and Asia. Specimens have been found in Java ('Java Man') and Zhoukoudian, China ('Peking Man'), but not in the New World. This was the first migration of hominins out of Africa. 'Migration' is the usual term, but may misleadingly suggest a planned movement of a whole settled group to a new predetermined settlement site quite far away. More likely is that regular nomadic cycles slowly shifted their range, with new places being visited more and more often, gradually pushing out the edges of the distribution of these hominins. *Homo erectus* probably made use of controlled fire, from about 1 million years ago, consistent with the beginning of reduced dentition and gut size, as cooking partially takes over the function of chewing and digestion. According to one theory, a reduced gut can be compensated for by a bigger brain, keeping the overall metabolic demands of the body constant. *Homo erectus* was the ancestor who shed his fur, leaving us relatively naked, over a million years ago. There is no completely satisfactory explanation for the move to nakedness. Possibly it helped keep the animals cool in the hot savannah, or perhaps sexual selection favoured a bare skin. The skin colour at this time may have been light, like chimpanzee skin under the fur, and quickly evolved blackness to protect against the African sun.

Clearly, *erectus* was a more successful species. Some of their success can reasonably be attributed to their living and working in cooperative groups, as they are believed to be the first hominins to hunt and forage cooperatively, roughly like modern hunter-gatherer groups. Advanced in-group cooperation suggests somewhat developed communication systems, though we cannot justify any claim less vague than this. The topic of cooperative hunting is fraught, as several other species, including modern chimpanzees, also hunt in groups. The issue is how much conventionally organized cooperation there is in the group; this will be discussed in Chapter 3. Beside being our own ancestor, *Homo erectus* was probably the ancestor of other later robust types, such as the Neanderthals (of whom more below), *Homo heidelbergensis* found in Germany, and Boxgrove Man from southern England, both dating to around half a million years ago. *Heidelbergensis* is associated with some large and exquisitely balanced wooden throwing spears dating from about 400,000 years ago, and also with even more ancient stone spear-tips found in South Africa and dating from about 500,000 years ago. Both types of spear show fairly elaborate planning, and spare time to carry it out.

There is complete consensus about the ultimate origin of our species in Africa, as descendants of the *erectus* living there. All agree that there was a first migration out of Africa by *erectus*, probably a trickle starting as early as 1.8 million years ago and ending as late as 800,000 years ago. And all agree that there was a much later wave out of Africa, around 100,000 years ago, or later, by *Homo sapiens*. For what happened when the *sapiens* incomers met the earlier *erectus* settlers, a majority view and a minority view exist. The long-held majority view, now challenged by DNA evidence, is that we modern humans completely eliminated the descendants of the earlier *erectus* populations who had moved out of Africa. Thus Java Man and Peking Man, for instance, are said to have no modern descendants; their lineages died out. This is the 'Recent Out of Africa' scenario. The 'recent' here is important, because nobody doubts that our earlier *erectus* ancestors came from Africa. Recent Out of Africa is a strong hypothesis, highly vulnerable to falsification. It makes an extreme claim: total elimination of one population by another. And it turns out, as we will see, that it is not tenable in its absolute strong form. The alternative, minority view is the so-called 'Multiregional Hypothesis', mainly pursued by anthropologist Milford Wolpoff. It is argued that there is enough similarity between *erectus* remains in Asia and the modern humans living there to conclude that the modern populations are in part descended from these Asian *erectus*. So the Asian *erectus* were not displaced by the new wave of *Homo sapiens* coming out of Africa in the last 100,000 years, but interbred with them. According to this view, there was some gene-flow between the earlier strains settled in Asia and later invading *sapiens* strains, fresh out of Africa. In this view, populations in Asia, Europe, and Africa were not totally isolated from each other during the million-year period we are talking about; there would have been sporadic contacts. Such contacts must have been rare, however, due to the sparsity of the population over vast distances. The relative homogeneity of modern human cognitive abilities is also partially explained, in this view, by parallel evolution converging on modern traits by independent natural selection in the different regions. The Recent Out of Africa explanation for the cognitive homogeneity is the more plausible one that these aspects of modern humanity were all present in a very small population that existed in Africa 100,000 years ago. It is not inconsistent to suggest that limited genetic intermingling with populations already outside Africa did nothing to upset the advantageous cognitive traits that had evolved inside Africa.

We don't know for sure whether it was biologically possible for Asian *erectus* to breed with incoming *sapiens*, but it doesn't seem unlikely, and if opportunities arose, then it probably happened. People don't need to like each other or live together to generate offspring. It is possible, even likely, that some genes that first appeared outside Africa, after the *erectus* exodus but before the later *sapiens* wave, have persisted into some modern human populations. The popular concept of ancestry, dominated by family tree metaphors, focuses too much on whole individual organisms and too little on genes. Evolutionary biologist Richard Dawkins has written: 'every gene has its own tree, its own chronicle of splits, its own catalogue of close and distant cousins . . . individuals are temporary meeting points on the criss-crossing routes that take genes through history.' Recent Out of Africa makes the strong claim that no modern human has any genetic material descended from the pre-100,000 *erectus* population living outside Africa. It is a highly falsifiable claim (a good thing in science).

For our purposes, concentrating on 'Why?' and 'How?' questions about the origins of language, we don't need to choose between these two competing hypotheses. The modern human population is indeed extremely homogeneous genetically, and no significant differences have been found between different populations in their inborn capacity to acquire complex language. Certainly there are individual differences between people within any given population, but nothing that correlates with a particular region of the world. Africans and non-Africans are born equally language-ready. A baby born anywhere in the world can be adopted in any distant corner of the globe by genetically very distant parents and will learn the language of its adoptive parents perfectly. So whatever genes contribute to the human language faculty, they at least would have been present in Africa before any relevant split by migration. On the whole, because of the uniformity of modern human innate language capacities, the Recent Out of Africa scenario is more attractive, for the relevant traits. But a relatively uniform language capacity across modern humans could conceivably be accommodated to the Multi-regional Hypothesis, and would imply that even at the *erectus* stage, a biologically given capacity for language was in place. It's not a claim made with conviction by any theorist, because *erectus* left us no fossil clues as to their communication skills, but it is a possibility, if a remote one. This all underscores the position that answers to 'When?' questions about language origins are beyond the scope of current investigation.

Genetics has an advantage over palaeontology, because we know that any modern DNA has ancestors, while we can't be certain, without invoking genetics, that any fossil has modern descendants. Recent genetic comparisons of people from across the world have shed interesting light on our ancestry. The clearest results come from mitochondrial DNA and Y-chromosome DNA, which are passed exclusively down female and male lines, respectively. Mothers pass their mitochondrial DNA (mtDNA) on to all their offspring, but only their daughters pass it on to the next generation. Sperms have far less mtDNA than ova, and whatever they have doesn't survive the fertilization process. In humans, paternal mtDNA is not inherited. Similarly, fathers pass their Y-chromosome DNA down only to their sons, and not to their daughters, because women have no Y-chromosome. This interesting genetics sheds some light on human ancestry, specifically on matrilineal and patrilineal ancestors, as I shall now outline.

For mtDNA, a large sample is collected from people all over the world, using individuals representative of populations who have lived in their region for a long time, e.g. Native Americans for the Americas, rather than people with Old World ancestry. This sample will show some variation, and the specimens can be grouped into subgroups and subsubgroups by similarity. Thus a family tree can be drawn for all the mtDNA in the sample, with each group or subgroup having its own branch or twig of the tree. The root of the tree will be a (perhaps hypothetical) specimen such that the smallest number of possible mutations lead from it to all the collected specimens. (So an outlier specimen with rather different mtDNA from many others in the sample is unlikely to be the root of the tree.) This root specimen represents the mtDNA of the purely matrilineal ancestress of all the other specimens. Some woman with that mtDNA was the matrilineal Ur-great-grandmother of all the people sampled, and the literature has provocatively called her 'Mitochondrial Eve'. The mutations from the Mitochondrial Eve specimen to the most distant specimen can be counted, and assuming a regular rate at which mutations in mtDNA occur, the approximate date and place at which Mitochondrial Eve lived can be inferred from the similarity of the root specimen to existing specimens from various parts of the world. A similar exercise works for the Y-chromosome, leading to a postulated 'Y-chromosome Adam'.

Mitochondrial Eve has been dated to about 200,000 years ago, give or take 50,000 years, and her mtDNA is more like that of modern Africans than that of people from elsewhere. This strongly suggests that she lived in Africa around the time when *Homo sapiens* was emerging as a species. Y-chromosome Adam also lived in Africa, and more recently than Mitochondrial Eve, at around 100,000 years ago, give or take 40,000 years. The most likely date here puts this individual also in the period before the migration of *sapiens* out of Africa. This Adam and this Eve never met, of course. And they were not alone. It's just that their companions didn't pass any mtDNA or Y-chromosomes down to us.

Fascinating as these results are, they can be very deceptive. The results are so nice and clear because they avoid the complications of sexual reproduction. Mitochondrial Eve was only the purely matrilineal most recent common ancestor (MRCA) of modern humans. Likewise, Y-chromosome Adam was only our purely patrilineal MRCA. If you have researched your own genealogy, you may have been frustrated by the historical concentration on male-to-male inheritance, with less record of mothers, sisters, and daughters. Your real family tree branches out backwards in time to four grandparents, eight great grandparents, and so on exponentially until, way back in time, you could seem to have more ancestors than populated the Earth. Your family tree and mine, whoever you are, and whatever your background, almost certainly share at least one individual who lived only 5,000 years ago. Any two people on the planet very likely have a common ancestor who lived much more recently than the Adam and Eve we have introduced.

Nuclear autosomal DNA, i.e. all the other DNA from the nucleus of the cell (not the mitochondria) and not the sex chromosomes, represents a far greater part of our make-up than mtDNA and the Y-chromosome. There are many other genes, all with lineages of their own, some younger, but many older, than mtDNA or the Y-chromosome. We are particularly interested in any genes that play some role in the human capacity for language. One such gene attracting much attention in the last twenty years is called FOXP2. We will discuss details of the FOXP2 case in the next chapter, but here it can be noted that the modern human variant of this gene appears to play a crucial role in language. Modern people with broken versions of this gene, due to a deleterious mutation, have speech and language problems. It has been found that the modern human variant of the FOXP2 gene was also present in Neanderthals. So at least some of the genetic foundation for modern language ability was laid down before the emergence of our species—see below.

So what about the Neanderthals? Both we and the Neanderthals are descended from *Homo erectus* (or *ergaster*). According to estimates based on DNA, we diverged from the Neanderthals about half a million years ago. Our species is usually said to have emerged around 200,000 years ago, in Africa. The distinction between genus and species is not hard and fast, and sometimes Neanderthals are classified as a separate species with the tag *Homo neanderthalensis*, and sometimes as a subspecies with the tag *Homo sapiens neanderthalensis*. Purely for brevity, I'll treat Neanderthals and ourselves as separate species; when I write 'modern humans' I exclude the Neanderthals. In many ways Neanderthals were similar to modern humans, with quite advanced tools and caring, cooperative social organization, and they were resourceful enough to live in Europe during ice ages. Indeed, they favoured colder climates, not being found in Africa. Stones tools of a Mousterian type, characteristic of the Neanderthals, have been found in several sites on Crete, leading to speculation that Neanderthals built boats or rafts and were accomplished sailors. No actual corporeal remains of Neanderthals have been found on Greek islands. On migrating out of Africa, our own species seems first to have turned only rightward into Asia, and to have occupied Europe much later. Quite probably *Homo sapiens* eliminated the Neanderthals, not necessarily by warfare, but by competition for resources. Neanderthals had been living in Europe for at least 250,000 years before modern humans arrived around 40,000 years ago, and died out within at most 15,000 years of their arrival. The Neanderthal evidence dated nearest to the present is from Gibraltar, suggesting a last outpost in Europe against the advancing wave of modern humans. At the other end of the range, in Israel, there is evidence of Neanderthals moving into sites vacated by modern humans.

Our species did not eliminate all traces of the Neanderthals. Current theories attribute between 1% and 4% of the genome of modern Eurasians to a limited amount of interbreeding with Neanderthals, during the short period of their overlap in Europe and western Asia. This is not surprising, given our modern experience of competing groups. To give a concrete analogy, this would be like tracing your genealogy back six generations to find that 31 of your 32 great-great-great-grandparents came from the same ancestral stock, and that just one had a different genetic background; this would give a contribution slightly over 3% to your genome from the untypical ancestor. Transplant this example back to a period between 50,000 and 100,000 years ago, repeated sporadically during contacts between Neanderthals and our own species (probably in the Middle East), but always with the proportions around 50 to 1 in favour of modern humans. This illustrates more concretely the very limited extent to which modern non-Africans are descended from Neanderthals. Specifically Neanderthal genes are not found in modern African populations.

Recently another strand of the hominin lineage has been found in the remote Denisova cave in the Altai mountains of Siberia. Only a finger bone, a toe bone, and a couple of teeth dating from about 40,000 years ago have been found. Amazingly, it has been possible to extract analysable DNA samples. And this DNA gives mixed results. The mtDNA differences between Denisovans, modern humans, and Neanderthals suggest that Denisovan *Homo* diverged from Neanderthals and modern humans about a million years ago.

A comparison of nuclear DNA suggests a rather more more recent divergence, around 700,000 years ago. The Denisovans left far fewer remains than Neanderthals: the only evidence we have for their existence is from this one cave. But they did exist, and DNA studies suggest that a small proportion of their genes survive in some modern human populations in south-east Asia and Melanesia.

Not very long (in evolutionary terms) after *Homo sapiens* emerged as a distinct species, we started wearing clothes. Modern human body lice live in clothes, not in hair, and DNA studies can date the genetic divergence of body lice from head lice to as recent as 170,000 years ago. Before that, humans and all their ancestors went naked. The adoption of clothing marks a significant moment in the emergence of culture. It is likely that the first clothing was not for keeping warm, as these people were still in Africa, but carried information about the status of individuals, much as robes, for example, later on carried prestige. As some of our *sapiens* ancestors moved to temperate latitudes, the African black skin of later *erectus* mutated to paler colours, allowing more synthesis of vitamin D.

Modern humans are clearly a very successful species, now numbering over 7 billion and occupying almost every part of the world. Interestingly, modern humans probably arrived in Australia, at least 40,000 years ago, before they arrived in Europe. There is debate as to when humans first colonized the Americas, with suggested dates between 40,000 years ago and as recent as 15,000 years ago. The Pacific islands were settled much later. Wherever humans have gone, we have made a significant impact on the environment. This is certainly due to our highly cooperative cultures and capacity for complex hierarchical thought. It must be assumed that in all these ways we far outstrip any ancestral species.

There is a school of thought that claims a further significant evolutionary change after the exodus of *sapiens* from Africa. This is sometimes called the 'Upper Palaeolithic Revolution'. In the debate we see a distinction made between 'anatomically (or skeletally) modern humans' and 'behaviourally modern humans'. More complex behaviour in the form of more refined and task-specific tools, and carved and painted art, certainly did come on the scene after about

45,000 years ago, and after some parts of the world had been reached by modern humans; the bow and arrow was invented around 30,000 years ago, and the first flutes, found in Germany, date from just a few thousand years earlier. Some researchers have suggested that this increase in cultural complexity coincided with the advent of fully modern language. A spurious connection has been made via the term 'symbolic'. Personal ornamentation such as beads, and rather abstract decoration of blocks of ochre are symbolic, in one sense of the term. Words in a language, however, are symbolic in a different sense of the term. So one cannot identify the advent of such art with the advent of language. In modern times, wall painting, carving of figurines, making of bead ornaments, and possession of elaborate stone tools are found in populations with fully modern language. But the absence of such features does not necessarily indicate absence of complex language. Some groups with fully modern language have no tradition of visual art: Nilotic tribes of Sudan have been cited as examples by anthropologist Jeremy Coote. These people don't make 'art objects', which is not to say that they have no common standards in visual aesthetics, like, for example, what constitutes a beautiful cow. The Foi tribe of Papua New Guinea have no graphic art, but have well-developed song poetry, according to anthropologist James Weiner. Future archaeologists excavating the remains of these tribes would be wrong to infer, on the basis of the absence of artistic artefacts, the absence of complex language. It is not clear whether the behavioural innovations of the Upper Palaeolithic were due to a biological change, as some have claimed, or whether they were spread culturally. The implication of some claims is that modern humans vary regionally in biological ways that affect their cognition, on account of mutations that happened only in some geographical areas. Focusing on language, there is no evidence of any difference in language-readiness between people in different parts of the world. It is likely that anatomically modern humans possessed complex language before this wave of behavioural modernity arose, given their success in colonizing the world.

From the Australopithecines through *Homo habilis* and *erectus* to *sapiens*, there has been a steady increase in brain size and cognitive capacity. Gross brain size is less important than the ratio of brain size to overall body size, and some measures emphasize particular parts of the brain, such as the prefrontal cortex. Modern apes generally have a greater brain to body ratio than other mammals, so the increasing trend started long ago, before the Australopithecines. Humans have the largest brains relative to body size of any animal. The human increase is more marked in several areas, including the prefrontal cortex, the cerebellum, and the white-matter cabling that makes long-distance connections between brain regions. There is no single area that can be localized as the sole seat of humans' unique abilities, including our language faculty. The principal parts of human brains are structurally similar to other ape brains; all that is different is the proportions of the parts, and the functions of some parts. In the human brain, Broca's area, a small region in the lower left frontal cortex, plays a role in language production, especially grammatical organization. There is an analogue of Broca's area in monkey and ape brains, but obviously it has no linguistic function. In macaques, the analogue of Broca's area plays a role in visual/manual imitation.

There are some interesting correlations with brain size. In primates generally, brain size correlates well with the typical size of a social group, as psychologist Robin Dunbar has shown. In modern humans, neuroscientist Ryota Kanai and co-workers have found a correlation between the number of contacts in a social network and the amount of grey matter in certain brain areas known to function in social cognition. Brain size also correlates well, among apes, with the occurrence of tactical deception, as psychologist Dick Byrne has shown; you need a certain calculating power to be able to outwit your competitors, including by deception. An indirect correlation between brain size and complexity of a communication system is also seen among primates in the correlation (established by psychologists Karen McComb and Stuart Semple) between the size of a social group and size of the repertoire of calls.

It should be clear that, along with all researchers in this field, I am using 'language' to refer to something unique in the modern world to our species. Popular phrases like 'the language of animals' extend the term confusingly, blurring enormous differences between language and other animal communication. All animals communicate, but only humans have the elaborate learned systems that we call languages. No animal communication system is on a par in complexity or expressive power with any human language.

Why did language only evolve in one species? This is sometimes posed as if it were an especially challenging question for language evolution. It is not. Why did very long prehensile noses only evolve in elephants? Why did very long necks only evolve in giraffes? Many species have unique traits. One of ours is language. A riposte might be that language is so advantageous that it would be surprising if only one species had taken advantage of it, so again 'Why only us?' Well, maybe humans just happened to be the first species to evolve language, and others might be expected, in the fullness of time, to take the same evolutionary path. After all, full language is very new—only half a million years old at most, and perhaps much younger. Give other species time and they might follow. But then, will humans let this happen? The signs are that our adventurous competitive species will try to make a home almost anywhere in the world, and is willing and able to use up any resources and eliminate any potential competition. It may be a short-term strategy, but in the short term it has worked for us, agents of mass extinction that we are. We seem to have polished off the Neanderthals. At least one tiny community of Denisovans lived into the era of modern humans and then disappeared. And the lately discovered *Homo floresiensis* (we don't know how closely related to us they were) didn't survive to coexist with modern Indonesians.

Our species spread across the planet in small groups, dividing and re-dividing and becoming spatially separated from each other as they kept penetrating new virgin territory. Groups developed their own cultural traditions, including their languages. The languages of the world became extremely diverse through this thin spread and geographical isolation of small populations. Historical linguists have managed to reconstruct family trees of some groups of languages. The best-known example is the Indo-European family of languages, with its subfamilies including Germanic languages,

Romance languages, Slavic languages, and Indic languages. There are enough similarities in the core vocabularies of these languages to convince us that a single mother language once existed somewhere on the boundaries of Europe and Asia, over 5,000 years ago. But beyond that distance in time, the trail goes cold. All attempts to draw deeper family trees of the languages of the world are highly controversial. There are over twenty major language families, on a par with Indo-European, and there are no credible proposals for how they may be historically related. For example, the early classification of African languages into four major families by the linguist Joseph Greenberg is now widely disputed, and his analysis of native languages of the Americas into just three families was highly controversial from the start. Current estimates put the number of living distinct languages at over 7,000. It is likely that in prehistory, even though the human population was much smaller, the number of languages was greater. The number of different languages that have ever existed is far greater than the number we can count now. To grasp this, we have to abandon the notion of global languages like English, Chinese, and Arabic, spoken by millions. Many of the languages of the 7,000-odd still found are spoken by very small isolated communities, numbering only a few thousand people. Most of these 'little' languages will die out in the coming century, leaving us with a picture of languages that is quite atypical of the situation that has existed for most of the 100,000 years since we began to have languages. From the start of historical times, we have been losing linguistic diversity fast. And, as we will see in a later chapter, civilization and now globalization have actually begun to make modern languages rather different in kind from the sort that was predominant in prehistoric times, when small bands of hunter-gatherers were colonizing the corners of the earth.

What above all singles out languages from other animal communication systems is their enormous semantic productivity. It is sometimes claimed that the human language capacity arose abruptly, giving rise immediately to unbounded combinatory possibilities. A more plausible alternative, considering the way in which evolution usually works, is that there was some degree of gradualness in the evolutionary process. Even today, language is bounded, as the sentences people use are all shorter than some fuzzy maximum length, due to limits in our short-term memory and processing powers. Let's be clear about how I'm using the term 'gradual'. In the span of life on earth, some 4 billion years, the rise of *Homo sapiens*, no more than 200,000 years ago, seems like an instantaneous event. During the roughly 1 million years in which African *erectus* was around, it is likely that there was an increase (perhaps steady, perhaps punctuated) in short-term memory and powers for processing sequences, already paving the way for easy management of the highly productive systems we see in modern human languages. And the cultural rise of humans was also gradual. We posit successive stages, such as the Stone Age, the Bronze Age, and the Iron Age and we know that these phased into each other over different periods and at different places. Hunter-gatherer cultures preceded pastoral cultures, which preceded agriculture, which came before industrialization. And shifts from one culture to another were not abrupt. Intermediate stages existed in which a group practised some pastoralism but also did some hunting and gathering. Even so drastic an 'event' as the Industrial Revolution, seen in the perspective of the history of life on earth, seems like a single moment; but we can trace the succession of inventions and technologies composing it in a timeline, and even give dates to these crucial moments. The rise of human language may have been very fast, but like the emergence of modern human culture and the Industrial Revolution, it can't have been literally instantaneous. It's hard to imagine it taking less than a few centuries. This being so, it is possible to theorize about the successive stages involved in the rise of language.

2

Nature, nurture, and language

Genes and culture

Genes and culture both pass information from one generation to the next. Genes do it silently, invisibly and, until recently, wholly mysteriously. Your mother and father pooled and shuffled their DNA to make part of what you are. Some of what you are is immutably genetic, aspects of your bodily features, such as your hair colour, your blood type, and your susceptibility to some diseases. What you are also includes your behaviour, and some of this too is dictated by the genes that you inherited, such as what makes you sneeze, and whether you can roll your tongue in a certain way. All of this is your biological 'phenotype', the sum total of your physical form and behaviour attributable to your genes, your biologically heritable 'genotype'. The culture you were born into also makes part of what you are, such as your religious convictions and the languages you speak. But you couldn't have picked up these culturally inherited traits without a platform provided by your genes. Only humans can learn complex languages, and this is due to our unique genetic inheritance. The language we hear in people talking around us was made by a combined contribution of their genes and their culture. To a large extent, we can disentangle the strands of the two contributions. We can see the cultural continuity between the specific language or dialect of one generation and the next. And we can identify the genetic dispositions that make us, as humans, 'language-ready' when we are born. We don't just ask, 'What, in detail and with as much precision as possible, is the language faculty?' We also ask, 'How could the language faculty have got to be that way?' It is a reasonable assumption that human language, obviously advantageous to our species, was helped to evolve at least in part by its usefulness, i.e. by natural selection. Discussion of the non-cultural dispositions to language-readiness is mostly in Chapters 3, 4, and 5 of this book, while Chapters 6, 7, and 8 discuss the cultural evolution of languages.

The origins to be considered here are not the origins of particular languages, such as Albanian, Zulu, or any of the other thousands of modern languages. This book will not trace the origins of French, for example, in Vulgar Latin, or how Latin itself originated in a postulated earlier mother tongue that we call Proto-Indo-European. These are all fascinating matters, the stuff of historical linguistics, which studies changes in languages over the last 5,000 years at most, and usually much more recent language changes, such as the Great English Vowel Shift of the fifteenth century. Such changes were all culturally mediated, the result of one generation adopting a slightly different version of language, for various reasons, including some kind of convenience, or even just fashion. Here, we try to probe much deeper into the past than historical linguistics can, and will consider biological changes in the species as well as cultural shifts in particular languages. We will assess what genetically determined changes must have occurred in the descent of our species to make humans able so readily to pick up the cultural artefacts, languages, that our communities hand down to us. Some of these changes happened gradually over millions of years in our primate lineage; more recent ones may have happened less than half a million years ago and had faster-acting and further-reaching effects.

One gene that has certainly played a part in making humans language-ready is the 'FOXP2' gene. This was discovered after research on a London family (the 'KE' family), about half of whom had a clear genetically inherited language disorder. Early publicity centred on the grammatical problems of the affected family members. They had more trouble than their unaffected relatives in adding certain suffixes to words in speech, like the plural -s and the past tense -ed. They were also generally less good at judging the grammaticality of sentences presented to them. In fact, the grammatical deficits are less salient than the clearly problematic pronunciation of the affected members of the family. Videos of these people talking make it obvious that a primary impairment is phonetic. They have orofacial dyspraxia, a condition severely impairing motor control of the lower parts of the face, so it's not surprising that their pronunciation is affected. An argument that the deficit is a specifically linguistic one, i.e. not a consequence of more general cognitive problems, is that the affected members of the family have IQ values in the normal range. This is true. On the other hand, it is also true that the average IQ value of the affected family members is significantly lower than the average IQ of their unaffected relatives. This latter fact argues in favour of some linkage between language proficiency and other cognitive abilities. The brains of affected family members have also been examined, revealing abnormalities in the size and functioning of some parts.

Since the discovery of the KE family, there has been wonderful progress on the genetic side. Over a few years, the source of the deficit was narrowed down to a mutation in a single DNA nucleotide base— that's one in over three billion bases in the human genome. Such a tiny change in the DNA makes a big difference to the phenotype, in this case. The relevant mutation was traced to the grandmother of the KE family. Roughly half of her descendants, regardless of sex, had inherited this single-point mutation, located on chromosome 7. Many mutations are neutral, not affecting the amino acids and proteins coded by the genes. But this particular mutation had the effect of substituting one amino acid for another, resulting in a slightly different protein in the body. This protein, known generically in its various forms as the FOXP2 protein, has complex effects on a range of other proteins and genes during the developmental process— effects which are still slowly getting unravelled by researchers. The human version of the FOXP2 gene differs from the chimpanzee version by mutations causing two amino acid changes unique to humans. The dates of these mutations can be roughly established as within the last million years, and it is clear that there has been positive selection for this mutated version of the FOXP2 gene. So it must have been doing something useful, and its role in language is an obvious candidate. As noted in the previous chapter, Neanderthals had the same variant of the FOXP2 gene as modern humans. Thus the phenotypic effects of this language-related gene were present in some form in the common ancestor of humans and Neanderthals, about half a million years ago. For clarity, it is important to note that many other species, including mice, bats, and birds, have some version of the FOXP2 gene, which expresses a version of the FOXP2 protein in them. In mice and songbirds there are intriguing connections to vocalization, as yet quite unclearly related in any obvious way to human language. FOXP2 is certainly only one of many genes affecting language. It happens to be the first we can pin down to a specific mutation.

Though biological and cultural inheritance are separate mechanisms, they can interact. Genes are selected on the basis of the advantages they give to individuals in particular environments. Species adapt to their environments. But species also change their environments, and then adapt to the changed conditions. This is labelled 'niche construction', and applies very saliently to humans. It is known that changes in cultural practices can trigger differential selection of genes. A well-known example of such gene-culture co-evolution is the biological adaptation to better digestion of milk products (lactose tolerance), following the growth of cattle herding in some communities. This biological adaptation to a cultural practice has happened within the last 15,000 years, in different pastoral populations and in several different biological ways.

Another example of gene-culture co-evolution, closer to language, is the relative smallness of our teeth. Chimpanzees have huge teeth compared to ours. Human teeth have shrunk in size since the split with chimpanzees. It is very plausible to connect this change with the cultural practices of cooking and grinding food. Cooked or ground food needs less chewing. The reduction in teeth size, then, probably happened quite late and fast in our evolution, starting with the use of fire, probably by *Homo erectus*. Interestingly, the trend toward smaller teeth has continued until modern times; this may be physical evolution still catching up with cultural evolution. The advent of cooking is also thought by some to have allowed the increase in human brain size, because a smaller gut required less metabolic energy, and the energy saved was reallocated to brain maintenance. These are all examples of the effects, direct and indirect, of cultural practices on the biological evolution of the physical phenotype—our observable appearance and behaviour. Those changes affecting teeth size and brain size relate to the evolution of language.

The most radical case of gene-culture co-evolution involves our phenotypic behaviour, rather than just the shape of our bodies. The behaviour in point is our constant talking to each other with words understood as carrying meaning, i.e. language, not just diverse uninterpretable noises. The advent of communication through conventional arbitrary symbols (simply, words) radically changed the environment in which humans lived. Humans constructed for themselves a 'symbolic niche'. Now, one person could say something to another, resulting in behaviour agreed and anticipated by both a few days' march away. And newborn babies now had a fresh challenge: to learn the symbols that their group had started to use, that is, to fit into a culturally constructed niche. The advent of learned symbolic communication, much the same as the advent of significant culture, brought about changes in human minds, lives, and societies far more radical than the recent advent of computers and the internet, impressive though that is. It is reasonable to suppose that humans adapted somewhat gradually to functioning in a niche partly defined by symbolic culture. At some stage after the first words were used, we also became capable of stringing them together in complex hierarchically structured sequences, requiring further advances in mental capacity. Beside being biologically based, complex language is a feature of complex culture. The advantages brought by complex culture keep the faculty for complex language going. We can't tell how fast was the spread of biological traits facilitating the learning and efficient use of words standing symbolically for concepts. The speed of the change may have been as fast as, or slower than, the spread of lactose tolerance in cattle-herding groups, which has been very rapid. And the spread of these final genes enabling language-readiness affected all of humanity. In the parlance of evolutionary biology, the language-facilitating genes went to fixation in the human population. We can all do it, barring a tiny minority of pathological cases, the result of trauma or adverse mutations.

Don't worry that this study will get fearsomely technical on the genetic side. Not much is known about which stretches of the DNA strand help to build what aspects of behavioural dispositions. Mostly we will discuss the phenotypes, the actual body shapes and behaviours that we can compare, for example, between humans and non-humans. We can get clues to the origins of language-readiness from comparative psychology, i.e. by looking at what aspects of language-like behaviour, if any, can be found in other animals. No other species has the full set; only humans have language. But some components of language in the broad sense are found in many other species. We will see these as we go along, but here it is worth mentioning a puzzle. Our closest neighbouring species, the chimpanzees, bonobos, and other great apes, lack some traits necessary to language that are possessed by species far more distantly related. A notable example is vocal learning, the ability to learn to reproduce the vocal behaviour of other members of the same species. Chimpanzees don't do it. They produce similar vocalizations, but these are instinctive, not learned. Songbirds, much more remote from us than apes, learn their songs from models in a previous generation. Nature, it seems, lays out a menu of possible language-related dispositions some of which are adaptive even in the absence of others, just as birdsong is. The function of birdsong is to attract mates and announce territories. We will see other examples of language-like abilities in non-primates, such as dogs and other birds—abilities which have not been complemented in these species by enough other evolved dispositions to amount to a full readiness for language.

Some cultural processes very likely played a part in the earliest language evolution, after the first glimmerings of biologically evolved language-readiness. As mentioned, historical linguistic comparisons reach only a few millennia back in human history. In making such comparisons, historical linguistics has reliably identified some universal tendencies in language change which presumably were also at work even in the more distant past, earlier than the time horizon for language reconstruction that historical linguistics is confined to.

We will take advantage of these known tendencies to push much further back in time, to theorize about how the very earliest languages began to take on a shape recognizable as embryonic of the complex patterns we see in today's languages. The most important tendency across time that we can use as a signpost to an earlier state of affairs is a collection of processes known as 'grammaticalization'. Grammaticalization, as we will see in Chapter 7, is a kind of change in a language that generally makes it more complex. No modern language spoken by a stable community over generations can be regarded as simple overall, or primitive. Racist attitudes of the past assumed that peoples with simple material cultures had 'primitive' languages, but centuries of linguistic research have dispelled this illusion. Indeed, some linguists have insisted that there can be no such thing as a primitive language. But as soon as we ask evolutionary questions it is clear that complex languages didn't just jump instantaneously into existence. There must have been successively more complex stages, starting from some truly simple kind of system. A plausible story involving grammaticalization can be told about the earliest stages of the evolution of grammar. This story will be laid out in Chapter 7.

What is a language?

If we're going to discuss the origins of language, we had better have a clear idea what a language is. You might think we wouldn't need to ask. Don't we all know what French, for example, is? It won't do to say that French is the body of rules and vocabulary laid down by the Académie Française, a self-appointed authority. Such authorities are notoriously unable to enforce their rulings. French speakers continue blithely to import loanwords from other languages, especially English, and even their grammatical patterns change without the blessing of the Académie. A common answer is that French (again for example) is the sum total of behaviours by a big population mostly living in France. But that isn't adequate. French is spoken elsewhere, and some people in France don't speak French. And some French speakers hop around between different languages, slipping in a bit of

Arabic here and there, for example. And there are different regional and subcultural dialects. And people speaking French sometimes get confused in mid-sentence, so details of their behaviour are not proper French, as they would agree on hearing themselves. This all goes for any language, and in general the more speakers a language has, the harder it is to pin down exactly what such a postulated collection of behaviours is, because it contains more variation.

Separate nameable languages, like French, Swahili, Norwegian, and so forth, apparently exist. These are cultural objects, the result of people in a population (fuzzily defined) being drawn to speak like each other. Social centripetal forces make languages. Individual people in a social group form an idea, most heavily imprinted on them as children, of the language norms of the group, and try to conform. An ideal that linguists have settled on is dubbed the 'competence' of a generic speaker of the language. Competence is what it is in adult speakers' brains that makes them behave in the complex, typically socially conforming way that they do. The emphasis on the brain makes it clear that competence is not a property of a community, but of individual people. There is no 'community brain'. Fortunately for linguists, the centripetal forces in a community often make it practical to treat individuals as equivalent in their conformity to a language under study. But it should not be forgotten that this involves an idealization of the real state of affairs, in which individuals vary.

The language faculty manifests itself in the ability of children to become native speakers of a language who can make intuitive judgements about the grammaticality of sentences and what sentences mean. The object of concern to linguists, in this view, should be the 'tacit knowledge' that all normal adults have of their native language. Thus, competence as knowledge rather than behaviour is emphasized, and behaviour itself (i.e. people talking) is sometimes held to be impossibly messy to describe, because it contains errors, false starts, interruptions, and other confusing stuff. The alternative to drawing data entirely from observations of people talking is to rely on 'the intuition of the native speaker'. Speakers, typically the researchers themselves, make introspective, and fully conscious, judgements about whether or not sentences of theoretical interest are grammatical for them. This has definite advantages, as some genuine combinations in a language get aired in talk so infrequently that one might never observe them in a large corpus of collected utterances. But a reliance on conscious intuitive judgements has dangers as well, because it can involve extrapolation beyond simple examples to cases that are too complex for people in ordinary circumstances ever to use, either in speaking or in listening. In such cases, what some theorists count as being in the language includes sentences that are never (not just rarely) used, and even never could be used, because they are too complex. A notorious kind of example involves 'centre-self-embedding', examples like *Actors women men like idolize get rich*, or worse *Actors women men mothers spoiled like idolize get rich*. If you are of the same inquisitive puzzle-solving mentality as many linguists, you will be able to figure out, with conscious effort, and probably rehearsing the parts of these examples over to yourself, what they should mean. And there are agreed-upon answers, which is taken as vindication of this method of deciding what counts as part of a language. If so inclined, you can go on as long as you like, making up longer examples. Great fun. Linguists of a certain persuasion would count all such consciously generated data as genuinely belonging in the language. Linguists of the alternative persuasion equally vehemently reject such examples as being part of any human language. The crux of the matter is whether you take a language to be behaviour (actual and potential) in real language use, or a set of examples including those which you know from conscious introspection to follow the same principles as obvious and simple cases.

The issue arises because humans, uniquely, are able to introspect about their own behaviour, to talk about talk, and to think about thinking. When a linguist 'intuits' that such-and-such a sentence is grammatical, he is coming to a conclusion about possible behaviour, asking the question to himself, 'Would I, could I, say that?' Being able to make judgements and talk about the use of words comes logically after the potential use itself. I say 'potential' because one can reasonably make an intuitive judgement about a sentence that has never been used before (perhaps like this one, which is OK, isn't it?).

Conscious judgements about language, made verbally explicit, as linguists do, are based on the prior spontaneous use of language, so we should treat such judgements with caution, though it is impractical to do without them altogether.

In the course of the evolution of language, primary talk about everyday affairs, such as where the water is, who is the best hunter, and whether Mary slept with John, came before secondary talk about the words and sentences themselves. It is that kind of primary use of language that evolved first, and that we should be first concerned with. Actual behaviour is messy, because people get lost in mid-sentence and make slips of the tongue, but real language in use is not impossible to see great regularity in. It is indeed 'tacit knowledge' in speakers' heads that accounts for such regularity in their behaviour. The language of a community is inevitably fuzzy at the edges, because nobody conforms 100% to the norms. But a core of norms, for any language, does exist, and individual speakers tacitly know them. 'Tacit knowledge' is an acceptable description of what is in speakers' heads, making them behave in regular conforming ways, so long as one does not get carried away to extrapolating to examples that never could be used.

'Knowledge' is a risky term. I 'know' how to ride a bike and tie my shoelaces, but this 'knowledge' is hard to express in words. On the other hand, some knowledge can only be held in words, including scientific and theological abstractions. Maybe Albert Einstein at first intuited non-verbally that $e = mc^2$, but the rest of us only know this, as far as we know it at all, through the symbolic formula. The limits of tacit knowledge are in some ways broader and in some ways narrower than the limits of knowledge that can be made explicit in language.

I will briefly discuss here a different question: 'What is Language?' Here, the word is capitalized and without an indefinite article because this is a question, not about languages, like Turkish, Hungarian, or Xhosa, but about the inborn human capacity for language. Chomsky's provocative answer to this question is that the language faculty is a mental computational system for combining atoms of thought into more complex thoughts, purely for internal purposes, with no necessary link to public communication. This language-as-private-thought idea neglects what is to most people an obvious function of language, namely public communication, and it offers no solution to the question of why so much of language structure is adapted to communicating thoughts to others. Much of the complexity in languages arises from different ways of presenting information in contexts where different knowledge is shared between speakers. Think of the differences among, for example, *The house was struck by lightning, Lightning struck the house, It was lightning that struck the house, It was the house that was struck by lightning, What struck the house was lightning,* and *What lightning struck was the house,* and many more ways of describing the same worldly event. That kind of variety in sentences is part of what English is. All languages have such variant ways of describing the same proposition, depending on the contextual situations of the speakers and hearers. That's the way language is. The language-as-private-thought idea offers no possibility of explaining why it got to be that way. Further, when we think by privately talking to ourselves, we do so in the public language which we have learned to communicate with from our mother's knee. French speakers talk themselves through mental puzzles using French words and sentences, Danes do it in Danish, and Tamil speakers in Tamil. We often use a culturally acquired tool, a particular language, to help us think. The language-as-private-thought idea, which divorces language from its outward communicative expression (speech or sign), can't explain how we come to be creatures that use the particular language in which we talk to others as a mental prop in talking to ourselves. Evolutionarily, it is more likely that there was some symbiotic co-evolution of our communicative abilities and our ability to think complex thoughts. Thus, considering language in the light of its possible evolution gives us a more coherent overall picture of what we should take language to be.

In fact, languages show many signs of having evolved, in that they preserve archaic features alongside novel ones. This is sometimes called 'layering'. Languages show growth rings, like the rings of a tree. In the grammar of any given language one can identify some constructions and types of word which are ancient, and others which have crept into the language more recently. And ancient and recent features coexist in languages, just as ancient and recently evolved features coexist in biological organisms. For example, the alternations in English so-called 'strong' verbs, as in *drive/drove/driven* and *sing/sang/sung*, originated thousands of years ago, even before English was English, in Indo-European. But the regularization of some such verbs, as in *helped*, which used to be *holp* and *holpen*, was an innovation in progress at the time of the King James Bible of 1611, which varies between *helped* and *holpen*. Much of modern linguistics has focused on characterizing languages in the spirit of the question: 'What kind of thing, in as much detail and precision as possible, are languages?' This is a valid and reasonable question, as far as it goes. Considering languages in the light of evolution asks the further, and necessary, question: 'How did languages come to be that kind of thing?' Considering language in the light of evolution gives us a better idea of what exactly languages are, and what the human capacity for language is.

Instinct and learning

Some behaviour is clearly instinctive, and some is obviously learned. A newborn calf instinctively struggles to its feet and finds its mother's teat. Some instinctive behaviour involves simple motor responses to conditions, like the blinking reflex when air is puffed into our eyes. For more complex instinctive acts, like the calf finding its mother's teat, we hesitate to call them reflexes, and might call them 'voluntary', because they involve an effort to attain a goal. Instinctive behaviour ranges from simple to relatively complex. At the most complex end, one might talk of an 'instinct for survival' that carries an animal through varied vicissitudes as far as it can. A so-called instinct for survival has no single motor response: it can be reflected in running hell-for-leather or standing stock-still, making a loud noise or staying silent, all depending on the circumstances. These responses are usually mediated in the brain by neurotransmitter substances, such as norepinephrine, which plays a role in the 'fight-or-flight' response to stress. Less technically, emotions such as fear and anger are themselves instinctive. Any so-called instinct for survival is best broken down into a collection of instinctive sub-behaviours, which have probably evolved separately, though all driven by the same ultimate evolutionary imperative. Language behaviour is so diverse as to be comparable with survival behaviour, so this example warns us to treat a phrase such as 'instinct for language' with care. There are separate instinctive dispositions for different aspects of language.

Contrasting with instinctive behaviour is behaviour that is learned. Learning is acquiring different behaviours in response to events in the environment. Being capable of acquiring alternative behaviours is plasticity. We learn how to talk, listen, write, and read in different languages. There is an interesting difference between learning a first language and learning the same language as an adult. Hungarian toddlers pick up Hungarian without effort, but a middle-aged English speaker struggles and never fully succeeds at the same task. First-language learning is reasonably called 'involuntary', and adult attempts to learn new languages 'voluntary'. Some aspects of second language learning are easier than others. Learning native-like pronunciation is the hardest part, and seldom achieved perfectly; learning new vocabulary is not too difficult for an adult learner, given frequent opportunities for use; and mastering grammar is somewhere in between, with common constructions naturally getting assimilated better than rarer ones (as a study by developmental linguist Carol Chomsky showed). It is common to speak of a 'critical period' for language learning, accounting for the difference between infants and adults. Language learning comes naturally and easily to young children, and the ability tails off around puberty. More accurately, there are several different sensitive periods for acquiring different aspects of language. The sensitive period for acquiring native-like pronunciation ends quite early in childhood. Some children of immigrants into a community can be verbally fluent, with good grammar and vocabulary, but never lose traces of a foreign accent. For vocabulary, it is not clear that there is a critical period, as people can learn new words throughout life, though perhaps not as fast as children. The slowdown of vocabulary learning in later life is at least partly due to the common most useful words having been learned already, leaving less common and less useful words to be learned later only if the occasion demands. Thus, the relation between learning and any instinct involved in language is complex, and differs for different aspects of language. The child's 'instinct' to learn its first language can be broken down, like the so-called 'instinct for survival', into a group of instinctive, and interacting, sub-behaviours.

But isn't there a problem? If we call first-language learning 'instinctive', aren't we in danger of clouding the useful distinction between instinct and learning? No, and confusion is avoided by observing three basic points: (1) getting in a good place to learn, (2) learning biases, and (3) the relation between instinct and what is inborn. I'll discuss these in turn below.

First, there are involuntary drives, to carry out certain behaviours that put one in a state ready for learning. For example, babies (excluding deaf ones) instinctively coo and babble, lying in a cradle vocalizing and eventually making random syllables in a charming sing-song way. From hearing their own sounds and experiencing the movements of their own vocal articulators, they are able to learn a correlation between acoustic signals and speech motor movements. Children also have an instinct to follow eye gaze and pointing, with obvious benefits for learning words that refer to things. And a 'mind-reading' instinctive understanding of the goals of others, no doubt reinforced by sympathetic and cooperative interaction with caregivers, enables a child to learn the purposes to which various constructions are put—for example, the rough correlation between interrogative forms and posing questions, or between imperative forms and giving directives.

Secondly, no learning is bias-free, and any bias affecting learning is itself instinctive. The biases affecting learning any specific task can often be identified in a range of necessary background abilities and dispositions. For example, children are disposed to attend selectively to objects, and so are biased, early in their development, toward learning the meanings of words denoting objects, rather than words for whole events or states of affairs. Simple consonant–vowel (CV) sequences are easier to perceive and remember than more complex sequences, so there is a bias toward learning words with this simple syllabic structure. Human short-term memory for sequences of meaningful words is impressively good, and we have an instinctive bias to seek sense in what people say to us, these together contributing to a bias toward learning complex grammar (as far as our working memory for understanding sentences allows).

Some innate learning biases are not so readily identifiable with dispositions that just put the animal into a state facilitating learning. For instance, if songbirds are raised without an example of adult song, they produce garbled singing not recognizable as the song of their species. But this garbled song itself leads, if presented to the next generation, to a 'better' song. After about five generations of birds successively raised with the song of the previous generation, where the first generation in the sequence started with no exemplar at all, birds now sing a song perfectly recognizable as the song of their species. This is an example of 'iterated learning' over many generations, to be discussed in the next section. The birds' innate singing dispositions, while definitely needing an example to learn from, push them in a specific direction beyond the features of the example itself. As there are degrees of plasticity, learning biases can allow a lot of freedom in what is learned, or funnel the learner down a narrow 'canalized' path with few alternatives. Much birdsong is strongly, but not completely, canalized. In the extreme case, where there is no choice at all between different learning outcomes, i.e. no plasticity, we are back at a completely instinctive behaviour. In the course of evolution, behaviour can become more or less canalized, i.e. less or more plastic. Humans have evolved to be the most plastic species.

The third point clarifying the relation between instinct and learning is that we should not conflate instinct only with purely inborn drives. A behaviour not at first automatic can be learned in a deliberate way and practised until it becomes 'second nature'. Then it is reasonable to talk of a learned instinct—something learned becomes instinctual. The best-known example is of Pavlov's dogs, who acquired a reflex to salivate on hearing a bell. Furthermore, we can consciously learn to suppress or inhibit instinctive behaviour, as in processes of socialization. Suppressing one instinct can pave the way for learned behaviours in replacement. Adult learners of second languages must inhibit their first acquired instincts to use the words and constructions of their native language, and painstakingly practise building up automatic behaviour in the new language, as far as is possible.

Learning itself can be divided into social learning from watching other people and non-social learning by solitary experience. Social learning is based on copying the behaviour of others. Non-social learning is of the trial-and-error sort, in which a creature attempts on its own to solve a practical problem and learns to repeat its successes and avoid repeating failures. The trials in non-social learning may be random or driven by some insight into the problem. Some non-human animals have surprised us by inventing solutions to practical problems without social models, like a New Caledonian crow who made a wire hook to get food from a pipe, or Sultan the chimpanzee who put two sticks together to reach some food. Non-social learning does not require the presence of other members of one's group. Good solutions to practical tasks can be discovered by non-social learning, and then spread socially, as when a famous Japanese macaque named Imo found a way of washing the sand off sweet potatoes in water, and was soon imitated by other macaques at the river.

Evolving systems can't arise by social learning alone. Social learning enormously speeds up the spread of innovations, but innovations, by definition, are not imitation. For a system to grow in a community, like a language, there has to be some independent invention of a new behaviour by someone. This could be a newly coined word that catches on, or a new grammatical combination that others find useful once they have heard it for the first time. Such inventions need not be conscious; indeed, grammatical innovations rarely are. Someone just happens to put words together in a way that stretches the established patterns of use, and other people, probably equally unconsciously, start to use the new combinations. Fifty years ago, no

English speaker said, *I was like* [PAUSE] *Wow!* or *I was like* [PAUSE] *Get me out of here!* Instead, they would have said *I thought* to introduce their reported reaction. We don't know who first used the *I was like* [PAUSE] construction. Once this pattern was out there in the arena of use, social learning by others picked it up and passed it on. Now even some 70-year-olds use it—I've heard one.

Social learning need not involve solution of a practical problem. With a disposition to imitate, one can socially learn behaviours that have no obvious practical benefit. Or one can imitate with no intention of solving a practical problem, and later find that the behaviour is, after all, useful for something. Children—instinctively, it seems—sometimes copy the behaviour of their caregivers without knowing why the adults are doing what they do. I'll tell you about Eve, my daughter, in her second year. Seeing her parents tie their shoelaces, she waved her hands around her bare feet in a way similar to shoelace-tying, but without the laces, and achieving no practical end. Seeing her parents pruning roses with secateurs, she took the secateurs, still locked shut, and held them carefully up against a rose stalk for a moment, again achieving nothing practical. More pertinent to language, her first 'word' was [naanaa], spoken in imitation of her father saying *Night night* to her as she was put to bed. She just said it because it was what people said at her bedtime. This instinct to imitate, not necessarily with any insight into meaning, is characteristic of children, and serendipitously begins to initiate them into the language community. They start to become people one can hold a conversation with.

Imitation involves a 'translation' from sensation to action. Somehow sensory information coming through the ears or eyes gets translated into motor information sent to the muscles of quite different parts of the body from the sensory organs. The discovery of mirror neurons has given us some insight into the mechanism of this translation. Mirror neurons are a small subclass of brain cells which do double duty, relating both to input to the central nervous system and to potential output of the system. In themselves they are neither pure sensory neurons nor pure motor neurons. The discoverers, neuroscientist Giacomo Rizzolatti and colleagues, took readings from single neurons in macaques. These neurons fired both when the monkeys saw a human grasping a peanut and when the monkey itself grasped the peanut. The result has been cutely dubbed 'monkey see, monkey do', but in fact the doing is inhibited, as the monkey does not actually carry out a grasping action when seeing grasping. Nevertheless this same neuron is activated when the monkey grasps spontaneously. It is easy to see how mirror neurons could facilitate imitation of observed actions. We can't ethically isolate actual mirror neurons in the human brain, but neuro-imaging evidence points to the existence of mirror systems in humans, which helps to explain the possibility in principle of the translation feat involved in imitation. Humans are known to spontaneously, even unwillingly, imitate certain socially significant actions of others, like laughing and yawning. Hearing or seeing laughter tends to make you laugh. That's why TV comedy shows put in that irritating canned laughter. The tendency to yawn when others yawn exists in a weaker form. Mirror neurons involved in hearing have been called 'echo neurons'. I will discuss the relationship between speaking and hearing speech in Chapter 5.

The infant's disposition to imitate contrasts with chimpanzees, who are more prone to 'emulate'. This is a useful technical distinction made by psychologists, between 'results learning' and 'action learning'. Emulation and imitation are similar, but emulators try to achieve the same desirable goal as someone they have observed, without necessarily doing it in the same way. Imitators just more dumbly do what was observed. Experiments by psychologist Andy Whiten show interesting differences between chimpanzees and children. Both are shown how to open a box in a certain way to get a reward. The demonstrated way involves an unnecessary action, such as tapping the box first before flipping the latch. Chimpanzees seemed to realize quickly that this tapping was unnecessary and cut to the main business of getting the box open. Children, by contrast, tended still to do the unnecessary tapping action before opening the box. The strategy adopted by children was in a sense less intelligent than that of the chimpanzees. It is statistically true, though not an absolute difference, that children tend to imitate while chimpanzees tend to emulate.

Humans are excellent problem-solvers, by comparison with other animals, but practical problem-solving is not at the heart of our language learning ability. Learning to speak your language does not have immediate payoff, like washing the sand off a sweet potato, or getting food out of a pipe. Rather, children see the language game being played around them and have an inborn drive to join in the game as best they can, at first by simple imitation and later, though soon, by acquiring an insight into the meanings of what is said, and the benefits that can be gained from continuing to play the game. The instinctive bootstrap into first language learning is not any insight into how to solve a problem. Children get social reinforcement for playing the community's language games. Their first faltering moves are not internally calculated to get attention, or get food; their parents just attend to them and feed them anyway. By contrast, getting food is by far the dominant goal in other animals' problem-solving.

Iterated learning

The experiments with birdsong mentioned earlier explored the idea of iterated learning. This mimics the cultural process whereby one generation learns from the behaviour of a previous generation, and the process is repeated over many generations. Over the generations, as studies along these lines have shown, the patterns of use become gradually more systematic. This is even the case when the first generation in an experiment is artificially given completely random unsystematic data to 'learn'. In this situation, learners introduce some order of their own, while trying not to stray too far from the data they were given as an exemplar. The iterated learning process has been modelled both in computers and with real people learning language-like data, especially by linguist Simon Kirby, with many others. The iterated learning approach can apply to the emergence of any kind of culturally transmitted pattern, such as systems of pronunciation ('phonology') or of grammar ('syntax'). In the description below,

I will focus on the emergence of grammar systems in which there are well-defined conventions for putting words together, in such a way that complex meanings are expressed by combinations of smaller meaningful elements, words. This kind of grammar, which we take for granted in language, is called 'semantically compositional syntax'.

Computer modelling seems a dark art to many people, but it's actually quite straightforward. Computers process data, with programs. A computer doesn't 'know' what the data it is processing is about; it just pushes its data-representing code around according to the program it has been given. The key concept to grasp is that bits of code in a computer program can be organized so that their components and the relations between them are directly analogous to the real-world entities and their interrelationships that one is aiming to model. The relations between entities are often dynamic, with one thing causing another. Thus, in the biological sphere, DNA copying can be easily modelled by defining bits of code as standing for DNA strands, with their four nucleotide bases. Likewise, weather patterns can be modelled by code representing locations in space, with assigned properties such as temperature and humidity; the dynamic causal relations between adjacent locations, depending on their properties, must also be defined. Given this, a modeller can then set up hypothetical initial conditions as input data, press a 'Go' button, and watch to see how things turn out. That's the basic idea of computational modelling, and it has been applied to many different scenarios in language evolution.

We assume that semantically compositional language was preceded by a 'protolanguage' stage, with meaningful words but with no grammatical organization. In modelling evolutionary routes from protolanguage to compositional syntax, the programmer typically defines a population of some number of individuals ('agents'), a set of possible simple world situations that they might communicate about, and a set of possible signals. The simulated individuals are made to interact with each other by randomly selecting some world situation to communicate to another chosen agent, and then trying to communicate this with a signal. The receiving agent is able to remember (store in computer code) pairings of the 'meanings' and the signals received. The agents are attributed with the power to learn from their experiences and to generalize over them. A cycle of repeated communicative and learning episodes is set in motion, and the programmer sits back to watch the outcome. In the simulations of the growth of compositional language from protolanguage, the striking conclusion was reached that it doesn't take more than I have outlined above to arrive, after some simulated generations, at a population that now possesses both a shared vocabulary and a shared conventional compositional grammar. Compositional syntax has evolved!—not from nothing, but from nothing yet culturally shared, i.e. from a situation with no shared vocabulary and no shared grammar. The agents only share language-readiness, a set of inbuilt dispositions to acquire and propagate this cultural thing, the shared language.

This conclusion depends on some crucial properties of the simulated agents, such as an ability to conceive world situations, a desire to communicate, an ability to remember past communicative episodes, and an ability to invent economical ways of communicating, based on the remembered episodes. Early humans almost certainly had such abilities, if only in weak doses. The computer models show what you get if you start with certain well-defined conditions and dynamic processes simulating communication and learning. The assumed abilities of the agents can be debated, but actually they are pretty uncontroversial. The conclusion of the simulations is not at odds with ideas of a 'language instinct', shorthand for a bunch of dispositions leading to the emergence of language. Indeed, the programmers have simply made precise in computer code what such a language instinct might consist of, including an ability to combine meaningful forms into longer forms whose meanings are composed of the meanings of the parts. The dimension added by these simulations is cultural transmission, one generation learning from the behaviour of the previous generation. In these simulations, compositional syntax emerges gradually in stages. The advantage of modelling is that a programmer can inspect intermediate stages in the running of his program. In these simulations there are stages when individuals have acquired partially compositional grammars, i.e. some whole meanings are still conveyed unsystematically by random arbitrary forms, while signals for others are now composed from simple forms with simple meanings. By one generation learning from the behaviour of the previous, in stages, it can be shown how a conventional compositional code could have evolved in a community. It is a demystifying result, not denying crucial inbuilt abilities to humans, but adding the necessary dimension of cultural transmission. The simulations show that, given the crucial abilities, with even a small bias toward learning from the behaviour of others, over time (perhaps even a long time) a socially coordinated system of quite complex language behaviour is the outcome to be expected. The small bias could be evenly present in all individuals, or distributed unevenly across the population. Linguist Kenny Smith has shown that a mixed population with some language 'constructors' and some who are mere 'maintainers' of a system constructed by others can still lead to the emergence of a systematic language.

Computer modelling is always idealized and simplified, compared to the real world, and shows what could possibly have happened, but not necessarily what did happen. Recently, Simon Kirby and colleagues have conducted iterated learning experiments in the lab with real human subjects. Subjects in Generation 1 are asked to learn what they are told is a little language, but in fact is just randomly and unsystematically organized. Then they are tested on what they think they have learned, and their responses form the basis for what is taught to the next generation. This transmission from one generation of learners to the next is continued. After about ten generations, a systematically organized language emerges. Real people have a disposition to impose order on chaos, and over successive generations order emerges, in the form of systematic form-to-meaning pairings and compositional rules for putting them together. The 'languages' in these experiments are trivial by comparison with real languages, but the 'order out of chaos' conclusion is valid nevertheless.

3

How trusted talk started

Communication basics

All animals communicate in some way. I'll keep here to a narrow definition of 'communication' as behaviour that influences the behaviour of others of one's kind, and, further, in a way that these conspecifics respond to as if recognizing a communicative intention on the part of the sender of the signal. This is a lot to require, and immediately excludes much behaviour that is only communicative in a weaker sense. I'll briefly mention some of the excluded examples. The lure of the angler fish, 'designed' by evolution to attract prey insects, doesn't qualify under this strong definition of communication. Another example, excluded for the same reason, is the commands of a shepherd to a trained sheepdog. Among conspecifics, forceful shoving to get another out of the way doesn't count as communication in our sense, but a tactful nudge might count, if the nudger and the nudgee have built up a rapport allowing understanding of such nudges. In this case, the person nudged is not forced to move, but understands, in some perhaps unconscious sense, that the nudger wants him to move, and acts accordingly. Acting accordingly need not be cooperative. Moving aside after a nudge may be cooperative, or it may be selfish, to avoid something more hurtful than a nudge.

Within this definition of communication, there are many examples in the animal world, both aggressive and cooperative. We are interested in cases where the signal has become 'ritualized'. A classic example is the teeth-baring of dogs, a threatening act, interpreted accordingly by other dogs. In the prehistory of the canine teeth-baring gesture, it is speculated, a natural precursor to a biting attack was the baring of teeth. At first, teeth-baring would have been followed up by a genuine attack. Intended victims of such an attack would learn that teeth-baring was a prelude to aggression, and take defensive action. Now, the teeth-barer can see that when he bares his teeth, the other dog either submits or adopts a defensive pose, making a real attack either pointless or costly, so he doesn't follow through with a real attack. Thus a ritualized behaviour has evolved whereby an animal influences another by a signal which is tacitly understood by both. We are not necessarily attributing any conscious calculation to the animals, although this 'anthropomorphic' way of describing the ritualization of the signal is convenient. The explanation in terms of ultimate causes is that dogs who act 'as if' they interpret teeth-baring as a threat don't suffer aggression, and therefore are likely to pass on this disposition to their descendants; in parallel, and co-evolving, animals who bare their teeth but don't follow through with an attack save precious energy and avoid the cost of injury, so this behaviour also gets passed on to later generations. It is all probably completely instinctive, in this case; teeth-baring is not a learned behaviour.

Other behaviours which count as communicative by our definition are equally clearly cases of the co-evolution of two complementary dispositions: a disposition to send a certain type of signal and a matching disposition to respond in a way that is ultimately advantageous to both animals. The obvious class of examples is courtship behaviours such as the songs of male songbirds and the courtship dances of other birds. Alarm calls of many birds and monkeys qualify, too. To use a well-known example, vervet monkeys have (at least) three kinds of alarm calls, for leopards, pythons and martial eagles. The monkeys have evolved parallel reciprocal behaviours: make a 'bark' call when spotting a leopard, and run up a tree when hearing a 'bark' call; make a 'chutter' call on seeing a python, and stand on tiptoe and look at the ground on hearing a 'chutter' call; make a 'cough' call when seeing an eagle, and dive under the bushes when hearing the 'cough' call.

There is an important difference between the alarm calls and the mating signals. The mating signals are 'dyadic' in that they are just a case of the animals doing things to each other, without any possible reference to a third entity. The alarm calls, on the other hand, are 'triadic' in that they involve the sender doing something to the receiver (warning him/her), but also are about a third entity, the leopard, or python or eagle. Triadic communication is communication about something in addition to the two animals involved as sender and receiver. The food calls of chimpanzees and macaques, made when one animal finds food, are also triadic, being about the found food. In triadic communication between animals, we see the evolutionary seeds of reference in language, a topic to which I'll return in the next chapter.

Human language use has both dyadic and triadic aspects. There are some purely dyadic speech acts, in which the only significance is what one speaker does to another in making an utterance, with no ingredient of referring to or describing anything. The conventional greeting *Hello* is meaningful, but doesn't describe anything. In saying *Hello*, a person greets another, and that's all. In saying *Sorry*, a person apologizes to another. In saying *Goodbye*, a person takes conventional leave of another. These are all things that we do to each other with words. The vocabulary for such bare non-referring speech acts in any language is only a tiny fraction of the total, but every language has them. They are reflections of a basic feature of all communication, namely the sender doing something to the receiver. For language, the Oxford philosopher John Austin argued this memorably in his little book *How to Do Things with Words*. This book initiated a rich seam in thought about language, emphasizing how the meaning of any utterance is not just the worldly situation that it describes or assumes (its 'propositional content'), but also what the speaker does in uttering it (its 'illocutionary force'). This seam of thought is known as Speech Act Theory. If, for example, a speaker says *It's raining*, not only does this describe a situation with water falling from the sky, but the speaker may be giving a friendly warning, or teasingly rubbing in the correctness of his earlier weather forecast, or inviting shared rejoicing after a drought. Whenever we talk to each other, we intend to do something to our hearer. That is the point of (non-pathological) talking. And in this respect, human use of language is no different from communication of all sorts in the non-human world. Of course, the possibility of adding descriptive content to the message, with words that refer to things, gives human language a scope vastly exceeding anything in the communication of non-humans. What human language added to animal communication was huge potential for joint engagement of speaker and hearer with situations beyond themselves, in the world invoked by the language in use. And over the course of evolution, we came to have the capacity to learn the massive systems for doing it, i.e. individual languages.

All of the animal signals mentioned above are almost entirely instinctive and unlearned. I say 'almost' because there is a slight degree of learning the 'meanings' of the alarm calls in baby vervets. They are innately disposed to make the 'cough' call on seeing something up in the sky, including falling leaves, but learn progressively during infancy to narrow down the class of things in the sky for which they give the cough, ending up with the adult behaviour restricted to responses to eagles. As mentioned in the previous chapter, there is a continuum between totally instinctive behaviour and learned behaviour, and in the lineage of humans, and apes generally, there has been a progressive shift toward more learned behaviour. Instinct never goes away completely, of course, as learning is always guided by some instinctive biases.

An interesting category of learned behaviour has been labelled 'ontogenetic ritualization'. The term 'ontogenetic' shows that this happens during the development of an individual. I'll mention a couple of cases that are, in a limited way, suggestive of how learned communicative conventions can arise. The first case concerns the 'nursing poke' behaviour that grows up between a chimpanzee mother and her baby. The baby instinctively seeks the mother's nipple. The mother does not actively present her nipple, and her arm may get in the way. The baby pokes the mother trying to get at the nipple, eventually succeeding. After some repetitions, the mother responds to the poke by moving to expose her nipple, something she did not at first do. A convention has now arisen between mother and baby, whereby the baby just needs to poke the mother subtly, not forcefully enough to push her into position, and the mother responds by moving into the right position. A second case of ontogenetic ritualization is seen commonly in human toddlers and their carers. At an initial stage, a mother picks the child up by lifting him under the armpits. The child gets used to this and starts to help by raising his arms when he thinks he's going to be picked up. Later, when the child wants to be picked up, and the mother has not shown any intention of doing so, the child raises his arms, essentially saying 'pick me up'. This action is recognized by the mother and often enough the child gets picked up. A little communicative convention has arisen between mother and child, with both learning something from the early interactions.

In these cases of ontogenetic ritualization (OR) we can see one necessary but not sufficient element in the foundation of group-wide learned conventional communication. On the positive side, OR involves learning by interaction and the rise of a little convention. But still missing is any prospect of such conventions becoming group-wide, as they are only mother–child conventions, and furthermore one-sided, with the child always the signaller and the mother always the responder. And these interactions are still only dyadic, with the actors just doing things to each other with no attention to anything outside the pair involved. But it is important to note that in these cases we see a communicative behaviour arise through learning, unlike the courtship rituals of birds and non-human mammals, and displays such as teeth-baring. In the evolution of the human capacity for language, there was a transition from purely innate instinctive communication to learned conventions over which the communicators have a high degree of voluntary control. How could this have happened?

The first hurdle which must have been overcome is that the sender and receiver of a signal recognize its 'signalhood'. Ordinary oral sounds, such as grunts, cries of pain, sharp intakes of breath, heavy breathing, snorts, and coughs are just what they are, carrying no more information than that a person is grunting, crying in pain, and so on. How can a cough, for example, come to mean something more than a cough? We can take a clue from our modern habits. If you are wanting to enter a room, and a stranger is standing in the way, with his back to you, and if you don't speak his language (you're abroad), what can you do? In many cases, a discreet cough will do the trick. You don't overdo it by making it sound as if you are having a real coughing fit. In this case, the discreet cough signifies 'There is someone behind you making this sound'. Sure, a real coughing fit would have given the same information, but probably too much, signifying also that the cougher has a throat problem. That someone has a throat problem is a 'natural meaning' of a cough, in the terms of philosopher Paul Grice. That someone wants you to get out of their way is a 'non-natural meaning' of a cough. The very discretion of the cough separates it from its natural meaning, recognizing the intention of the cougher to communicate something, rather than just to cough. Here now we have two elements of the act—its similarity to a real cough, and its dissimilarity from a real cough—evident in its polite nature.

Anthropologist Greg Urban has described a case in which members of a community mourning a death want to express their grief, and simultaneously want it to be known that they are deliberately expressing grief. In this case, they make wailing sounds something like the natural sounds of distress, but different enough from them to be recognized as deliberate. Hearers know what the conventional wails mean, recognizing both the grief and the conventionality. Urban stresses that the conventional signal, unlike a spontaneous natural sign of distress, is under voluntary neocortical control; that is, there is some kind of deliberate calculation or intention involved. Similarly, the brain activity behind a real cough and a discreet cough signalling 'I'm here' is also different. A coughing fit is a reflex response to irritation in the throat; if anything, the only voluntary effort is in an attempt to suppress it. A 'signalling' cough, on the other hand, is voluntarily managed, with neocortical control. The same difference exists between spontaneous smiles and deliberate smiles—they are initiated by different parts of the brain, and the deliberate kind is a calculated signal, for example by a shop attendant or a politician.

I noted of the teeth-baring by dogs that the animals behave as if they were making a real calculation, something like 'If I bare my teeth, he'll think I'm going to attack him'. This is anthropomorphically, and no doubt wrongly, imputing mind-reading and manipulation to the dog. For dog teeth-baring, biological evolution has done the work, breeding in the specific threatening and submissive response behaviours, with no need for the animals to think about what they are doing. We humans thoughtfully and consciously mind-read and manipulate each other all the time, in both cooperative and competitive ways. 'Manipulation' here need not imply selfish exploitation; it can be to the advantage of the person manipulated. I recently saw a car driver preparing to leave a car park which I knew was full, and inferred that he had been looking for an empty slot and not found one. I waved, gestured at myself, pointed in the direction of my own car, and made a twirling motion with my hand. He understood that I was telling him I was about to vacate a parking slot. We were strangers to each other, and my gestures were not established conventional gestures. I read his mind and he read mine, and I manipulated him into a situation that suited him, and cost me nothing. (Why would anyone do this? See later on altruism.) This is a cooperative example of mind-reading and manipulation. There is a large literature in linguistics on 'implicature', a term introduced by philosopher Paul Grice to describe the indirect inferences we make from each other's utterances on the premiss of cooperativeness.

Much human communication rides on mind-reading, or at least mind-guessing. When two speakers converse about a thing, or even an abstract idea, they each have a similar representation in their head of the thing or idea they are talking about. In the most concrete case of talk about some object in the current situation, e.g. *The floor is wet*, both speakers end up sharing joint attention to the thing talked about. This is a prerequisite for any triadic communication. Mutual communicators need to be able to maintain joint attention to whatever is being communicated about for at least as long as the communication takes. A child's capacity for joint attention with a carer is helpful in learning the meanings of words. The better a child can attend to the things an adult is talking about, the more successful she will be in picking up the correlation between words and things. And in turn, once some words have been learned, the words themselves are helpful in drawing attention to other things mentioned in the context. Computer scientists Tao Gong and Lan Shuai have simulated a co-evolutionary spiral between an increasing capacity for joint attention and increasing communicative success with language.

A simple foundation of a capacity for joint attention is seen in the gaze-following behaviour of chimpanzees. If a human enters a chimpanzee's presence and looks pointedly at the ceiling, the chimp will look up there also. Often, too, if the animal sees nothing interesting on the ceiling, it will look back at the human's face to check whether he is still looking upward. This shows at least a superficial understanding of visual attention, and an interest in participating in another similar creature's attention.

We humans are exceptionally good at mind-guessing, but other apes can do it, especially in competitive, rather than cooperative, situations. There is plenty of evidence that chimpanzees have a 'Machiavellian intelligence', in the words of psychologists Dick Byrne and Andy Whiten. They scheme to their own advantage, calculating the likely behaviour of others in their group. An economical description of their Machiavellian ways attributes to them human-like mind-reading and some degree of understanding of the intentions and beliefs of others. Experiments by psychologist Brian Hare and others have shown that, in their words 'Chimpanzees know what conspecifics do and do not see', and even what others believe. So far, however, no evidence exists that an ape can attribute a false belief to another. That is, we humans can know that someone believes something which we know actually to be false. This level of sophistication in mind-reading has not been shown in our nearest relatives.

Using mind-guessing, we can even convey meaning by using anomalous sentences. If someone says to you *You're the cream in my coffee*, it may take some working out that this is intended as a compliment. What else could it be? you reason (unless you have an abnormal condition, such as autism, that resists all but the literal interpretation of utterances). Compare this with *You're a star*, which is now immediately interpreted as a compliment. But the original literal meaning of *star* was just a twinkling object in the night sky. Back then, any time before about 1800, an utterance of *You're a star* would also have taken some working out. How can a person, literally, be a pinpoint of light? The extension of the meaning of *star* has now been conventionalized, as part of the language code, to mean an outstandingly good person. This illustrates the dual nature of our understanding of what people say to us. Some of the work is done by straightforward knowledge of what words conventionally mean, the code; the other part of the work is done by inference, or mind-reading. In the history of languages, there is a trend for frequently made inferences to become conventionalized.

Competitive examples of mind-reading and manipulation are seen in deceptive feints and dummy actions in sports: a player acts as if preparing to make a certain move, and his opponent reads his apparent intention and acts accordingly, while the dummy signaller at the last moment performs a different action. Note that this example is from sport, where the normal rules of cooperation are suspended. Human everyday life is normally cooperative, at least within groups, but competitive mind-reading and manipulation, bluff and double-bluff, happens extensively in crime and war. In a competitive situation, there can be an arms race between ever more sophisticated levels of mind-reading and manipulation. Selling a dummy in football or rugby must be done with a certain subtlety, or it fails. A criminal who realizes he is being tailed by a detective will take measures to throw the detective off the scent. If the detective mind-reads this decoying action, he may alter his tailing techniques. Knowing that deception is a possibility encourages higher levels of mind-reading. There is an important difference between cooperative and competitive signals. In a competitive situation, more convincing signals require more effort and/or elaborate thought. To send a credible message in a competitive situation, a signal has to be costly. Cheap deception is easily seen through. Some behaviours are simultaneously cooperative and competitive, toward different interactors. The peacock wants mating, cooperation, from a peahen, and competes with other peacocks for the privilege. The peacock's costly tail results from a feedback loop in which peahens are attracted to ever more gorgeous tails.

This relates to language in the following way. Language signals are cheap to emit, though fairly costly to learn. And humans are simultaneously in cooperation and competition with other members of their social group. We walk a delicate tightrope maintaining trustful reciprocal cooperative relationships, while also making sure we are not taken advantage of and get our fair share of resources. The language code of a group is a tool for facilitating in-group cooperation, but to elicit cooperation, the tool is best used with good fluency and plausibility as a fellow group member. Statistically, language is overwhelmingly used for non-deceptive purposes; lying is the exceptional case. The complexity of language is not a defensive adaptation against the possibility of it being used for lying. Honestly and dishonestly used language can be equally complex. If anything, honestly used language, 'plain talk' expressing 'the plain truth', is simpler. The truthful cooperative nature of typical language use is consistent with the cheapness of speech and the reciprocal trust characteristic of human groups. The trust is not so easily bought, requiring years of apprenticeship while young in learning the code of the group. Research shows that humans are more trusting of, and likely to cooperate with, people who speak the same language, and especially with the same accent. (This is an instinctive response, and a particular neuromodulating hormone, oxytocin, is associated with social trust and bonding.) To some extent the complexity of languages is a signal of group membership, bringing with it an assurance that a speaker has gone through the appropriate initiation processes of the group. To be sure, some of the complexity is simultaneously useful for conveying complex messages, but any receiver of a complex message needs to assess whether the sender is trustworthy. People capable of learning the complex code of a group are accepted by the group. If a code were too simple to acquire, fakers could infiltrate the group. (In thinking about language in this way, we need to discount the highly artificial conditions of modern urban societies with extensive mingling of people from different original groups. To a first approximation, extensive contact between language groups leads to simplification of hard-to-learn aspects of languages, as we will see in Chapter 7. Conservative resistance to multiculturalism in some people is an ancient instinctive response that was adaptive in earlier times before urbanization, when people lived in small and generally quite isolated groups.)

One for all, and all for one

So we see the basis of human language in a disposition to communicate cooperatively. A species whose members were not minded to cooperate with others in their group would not evolve language. We humans often moralize regretfully about how nasty and vicious we can be. Certainly, human nastiness happens, and we have invented technologies for mass nastiness. It may surprise you to hear that humans, by comparison with other species, are conspicuously cooperative and helpful to each other, especially within a social group. Some interesting research comparing us to apes has testified to this.

Humans routinely point at things to draw attention to them, using an extended index finger or an outstretched palm, and in a few societies a chin or lower lip. Sometimes this supplements talk, as when we simultaneously say *that one*. But, especially in busy or noisy situations, we sometimes just point at things without the accompanying pronoun, and are understood. Children learning words are often helped by adults pointing at things. This is all part of normal cooperative language use. A remarkable fact about apes in the wild is that they do not point. Jane Goodall, in thirty years of observing chimpanzees in their native forest, has never seen a chimp draw the attention of another to an object by pointing at it. Nor has any other observer. In captivity, chimpanzees do point, but still not with other chimpanzees. It is just a behaviour they have learned with their human carers, and they use it only for requesting things. It is purely self-interested. Children, by contrast, often point at things, not with any intention of getting hold of them, but to share an interest. 'Look, a birdie', for example, might be the message that an adult draws from a toddler's bare pointing action. This could be a partial overinterpretation by the adult, as the toddler may not know exactly what adult category the object of interest falls in. But such willing and spontaneous pointing by a young child shows the first essential element of most communication in language, namely identifying what is being talked about. Developmental psychologist Susan Goldin-Meadow has noted very early communicative efforts by children consisting of two parts, a pointing gesture and a spoken word. In these children, this developmental stage is followed by a two-word stage, in which a spoken word now does the work previously done by pointing. Chimpanzees don't naturally even start along this communicative road, helpfully identifying something they want to give some information about.

Humans are helpful to captive chimpanzees, and the animals learn to benefit by pointing to request objects. But it is not reciprocal. Chimpanzees don't even seem to understand when a human points at something, as shown in a nice experiment by psychologist Michael Tomasello and his colleagues. This experiment contrasted a cooperative pointing situation with a physically very similar competitive grasping situation. In one condition a human experimenter reached through a hole in a plexiglass screen and made a pointing gesture toward a container, as if trying to communicate to the chimpanzee on the other side of the screen 'Look, something interesting in there'. Typically, the chimpanzee took no notice. It is as if he could not grasp that the human was actually trying unselfishly to help him by pointing at something that might be to his advantage. In the contrasting condition, the human experimenter again reached through the hole and made a grasping action toward the container, as if aiming to get something from it. In this case, the chimpanzee response was typically competitive, and he also went for the container, as if thinking 'Aha, something good in there—I'll get it for myself'. Chimpanzees, it seems, are able to mind-read the intention of a human experimenter, but only in the case where the human is intending what a chimpanzee would also naturally intend. A chimpanzee can understand a competitive state of mind in another, because he also habitually acts competitively. But a chimpanzee cannot readily understand an unselfish cooperative state of mind in another, because he typically is never in that kind of state himself. (Despite the pronouns in the above, there is no difference betwen males and females in these experiments.)

Aren't chimpanzee mothers, you might ask, generous and cooperative toward their offspring? Only to a limited extent. They do carry them around, but some of this is a matter of the infant grabbing the mother's fur. Female chimpanzees take a 'motherly' interest in the young of other chimpanzee females, as if wanting them for a plaything. Mothers do allow their babies access to a nipple, but later, when the young one is eating solid food, a chimp mother does not pass food to her young one, but just tolerates it scrounging bits and pieces from her.

Animals in experiments can be induced to cooperate with each other, but there needs to be an obvious reward. In one lab set-up, by primatologist Joan Silk, a food tray needs to be pulled near the chimpanzees' cage, if they want the food. The tray can only be moved if two chimps simultaneusly pull on separate ropes. They learn to cooperate in this way. These chimps are also able to pick better and worse cooperators to work with. But once the tray-pulling has been successfully achieved, a dominant chimp may selfishly grab all the food from his junior cooperator. Human cooperation, by contrast, is not always linked to immediate reward.

When the topic of cooperation in other species is raised, hunting by predatory groups such as lions, wolves, and chimpanzees is often mentioned. Chimpanzees hunt monkeys, tear them apart, and devour the pieces. For all lions, wolves, and chimpanzees, there is common attention to the prey. And the behaviour of members of the hunting group can be interpreted as if they are following a centrally coordinated plan. But are they? It would look much the same if each individual hunter animal joined in the hunt maximizing its own chances of benefit according to the whereabouts of the prey, and the current disposition of the other hunters. If one hunter chases the prey directly, it makes sense for the next closest to take a flanking approach, to right or left. And the third closest will, trees and other natural obstacles permitting, take a complementary flanking approach. Others will join in as the lie of the land and the precedence of other hunters allows. This is cooperation, in the literal sense of operating at the same time and place as others, and with the same goal. When the prey is caught, other conciliatory group attitudes take over and there is not usually an unseemly fight over the booty.

Group hunt settings are mutualistic, in the sense that the dice are loaded such that an individual acting alone will typically benefit less than if joining in an activity with others. In a mutualistic situation an animal attempting to act in concert with others benefits if the others also play their part, but does not pay a significant cost if the others don't play. Thus, mutualistic scenarios differ from the 'Prisoner's Dilemma' scenarios in which one player suffers a cost (of being 'suckered') if the other potential player does not cooperate. Not all ecological settings encourage mutualism. In some chimpanzee environments, it is easy for a lone hunter to catch a monkey, so little or no group hunting occurs.

There are different degrees of apparent organization of hunting in different species. Lions appear more organized than wolves, and chimpanzees more so than lions. Lion prides are more stable over the years than wolf packs, and individual lions are known to take habitual roles, as flankers or centres in group hunts, whereas individual wolves have not been observed in such habitual roles. There is some evidence that the roles taken by individual lions relate to their physique, whether stockier or more lithe. Now, compare a lion hunt with a bunch of unrelated humans informally gathering round a street performer in a city square. Each person stands where she can get the best view—not too close to the performer to cramp his style, preferably facing the performer's front if they get to the scene in time, and not behind bigger people. In humans there is also some politeness and deference, with shorter people being allowed nearer the front. This is a classic example of self-organization, with no central organization of who stands where. We cannot say whether one lioness, even an experienced one, in her individual role in the hunt, can understand that the prey will be blocked by other lionesses. She may simply be acting like a person watching a street performer, getting to the best position for herself, given the current location and direction of the prey. Even among lions there is occasional cheating, with animals who have not participated in a hunt nevertheless taking some of the rewards; the prevalence of such cheating is related to the ecological conditions in an area.

In some chimpanzee groups, but not all, hunting is more socially organized, and the degree of organization is related to the environment. For a lone chimp to chase a monkey in an area where the trees are not very high is easier than in dense forest with high trees. Only in the more challenging environments has highly coordinated hunting developed among chimpanzees, as primatologist Christophe Boesch has found. In the most organized group, in the Taï forest of Côte d'Ivoire, some individual animals learn, over as much as ten years, specialized roles in the complex activity of chasing a fast-moving monkey who can get higher up in the trees than the chimps can. Not all the chimps learn this role, and it takes a long part of the lives of those who do, from the age of about 10 to about 20. This degree of complexity in cooperative hunting is not characteristic of the whole species, and only emerges in challenging environmental conditions, as at Taï. The cooperation is, moreover, limited to this one task. This contrasts with linguistic cooperation among humans, which applies across many different tasks, is found in all populations, and does not involve particular individuals learning specialized roles. On the other hand, the example does show some continuity in evolution, as this is the most developed case of learned social teamwork, and it is found in our closest biological relatives.

Cooperation is closely linked to altruism, defined as behaving to the benefit of another creature but at a cost to oneself. Self-sacrificial behaviour is the extreme case of altruism. Humans are conspicuously altruistic, especially within a social group. Some altruistic acts require empathy, knowing how another creature feels in a hard situation. Seeing a person in pain does not induce actual pain, but it does trigger an understanding, based on one's own experience of pain, of what the other person is going through. Mirror systems, such as those involved in laughter and yawning, discussed earlier, facilitate this kind of empathy. Of course, it's one thing to 'feel another's pain' (as they say), and another thing to do something helpful about it, possibly at a cost to oneself.

Biologists have puzzled over how a motivation toward altruism could evolve, given that selfish behaviour would always seem to be to the best benefit of an individual's genes. And it's individuals who reproduce themselves, so altruism of any sort seems at first blush to be a challenge for Darwinian evolution. Self-sacrificers in their prime have fewer offspring. In fact there are several mechanisms, now well understood, by which altruistic behaviour can evolve, without undermining basic Darwinism. A mother who is disposed to care well for her offspring, at some cost to herself, will improve their life chances. The offspring will inherit the instinctive dispositions of the mother, so well-cared-for infants disposed to be altruistic carers themselves will prosper. A lot of qualifications need to be made, explaining why fathers are not so altruistic as mothers, and why offspring are not reciprocally altruistic to parents. Such details are straightforward. Paternity is not so evident as maternity; a father cannot be sure which kids are his. And mothers who have already had offspring, and passed on their genes, have less time left in their lives to benefit from any altruistic act than their offspring who have yet to get into the mating game. Such theories, labelled 'kin selection' and 'inclusive fitness', originated by biologist William Hamilton, explain the prevalence in nature of altruistic behaviour toward close biological kin. Humans are just like many other species in their altruism toward family members. This is a start, but only takes us a limited way to explaining the far more extensive altruism shown by humans, not quite to all and sundry but at least to biologically unrelated members of their social group.

In non-human animal life, social groups are often also groups of biologically related individuals, such as extended families, or clans. Humans form social groups in which membership is not defined by recent ancestry. There was a gradual transition from small groups with strong family ties to larger groups consisting of several allied and cooperating families. Eventually in modern times we have large social groupings of biologically unrelated people, definitely artificial and more or less ephemeral, like gangs, armies, religious sects, and trade guilds. The interpersonal relationships within such groups are characterized by reciprocal altruism, an understanding that helping another at some cost to oneself today creates a debt that one can expect to be repaid with help from the other in the future. The theory of reciprocal altruism was pioneered by sociobiologist Robert Trivers. The motto of the three musketeers, 'One for all, and all for one' captures the spirit of reciprocal altruism in a collaborating group. The principle has been called 'Tit for Tat', which also reflects its negative side, that a bad deed today can be expected to attract retaliation. The full and remarkably simple prescription of the Tit for Tat strategy is 'Help those who have helped you, and anyone you meet for the first time, and don't help a person who declined to help you in the past'. Social theorist Robert Axelrod has organized computer competitions showing that this is the most advantageous tactic an individual can adopt in repeated social interactions. This is even true in non-mutualistic circumstances where an individual actually pays a cost if he tries to cooperate with another and the other doesn't reciprocate, and the non-reciprocator gains a benefit by 'suckering' the attempting cooperator. These are so-called 'Prisoner's Dilemma' scenarios. Tit for Tat is successful because of its built-in memory of past collaborators and non-collaborators. Once bitten by a non-collaborator, you never give that person the chance to harm you again.

Reciprocal altruism functioning within a group requires certain advanced cognitive traits, including memory for past good and bad deeds, some way of recognizing members of one's own group, and mechanisms for detecting and punishing cheaters who take the benefits of group membership without paying their dues by occasional altruism. Now computer scientist Luke McNally and colleagues have modelled the growth of a network of neurons from extremely simple beginnings to more complex networks correlated and co-evolving with a steady increase in the degree of cooperation between individuals in an iterated Prisoner's Dilemma scenario. The increase in cooperation was not built into the simulation, but evolved as individuals who benefited from the cooperation of others tended to have more offspring. And just those individuals also developed larger neural networks. The networks were effectively keeping track of the interactions with other individuals.

There are some slight traces of reciprocal altruism in non-human animals, such as limited short-term food sharing among chimpanzees, and mutual grooming. But humans stand out as far more reciprocally altruistic than other animals. The progression from altruism among close kin, common in animals, to the rare and characteristically human reciprocal altruism is reflected in the kin terminology of many tribes even today. In such tribes, a single word denotes one's mother and all her sisters; and another word denotes one's father and all his brothers. The obligations of close kin such as parents and siblings are stretched by the linguistic usage of the group to include uncles, aunts, and cousins. In urban societies, important social groups with no biological relatedness (other than being within the same species), such as religious orders and trade unions, also use the kin terminology, with members referred to as 'brothers', 'sisters', 'mothers', and 'fathers'. The naturalness of altruism to close kin is extended to artificially maintained groups by language. Marital conventions, also firmly entrenched in human societies, stretch the bonds of reciprocal obligation beyond kin, and link families in alliances. Language plays a part in maintaining such social structures, beside its instrumental function of aiding collaboration on group tasks such as hunting and moving camp. What else could possibly bind together an enduring group of unrelated people, other than expressions of unifying custom, purpose, and destiny in a shared code, a language? As the expressive power of language evolved, so did its potential strength in forming social groups reaching beyond the bounds of close kin. Somehow, humans alone made this transition. It was adaptive, in that members of collaborating groups benefited from the overall successes of a group in competition with other groups. Perhaps the feature of competition with other groups also accounts for the uniqueness of this kind of highly developed social arrangement in humans, for humans have ruthlessly outcompeted other species with less cohesive group action.

4

Concepts before language

Meaning is no mystery

Most of the time, we try to say what we mean. And our hearers try to work out what we mean from the stream of sounds that hit their eardrums. We can picture what happens by saying that speakers and hearers use a language system (such as English, or Swahili, or Japanese) to cross a bridge between meanings and speech sounds, and vice versa. A speaker crosses the bridge in one direction, starting with some intended meaning in her head and then producing an appropriate spoken utterance; and a hearer crosses the bridge in the other direction, taking in the acoustic signal from the airwaves, and figuring out what the speaker's meaning was. English speakers and hearers use the English bridge, Arabic speakers cross between meanings and sounds by the Arabic bridge, and Dutch speakers by the Dutch bridge.

These bridges are of course figurative. Real bridges connect solid physical places to each other, like Brooklyn and Manhattan. Speech sounds, at one end of a language bridge, are also clearly physical, events which we can record and measure with instruments. But meanings, whatever they are, are not physical in the same way. Nonetheless we can safely start with the assumption that when a person says something like *The car is just around the corner*, it is triggered in his head by something different from what would have triggered, again for example, *I love you*. This triggering state of a person's mind is our entry point into discussing meaning. I have just used the words 'head' and 'mind' somewhat interchangeably. Now let's bite the bullet and for present purposes frankly talk about brains. 'Mind' is what goes on in the brain, and the brain is in the head, where we can, especially now with modern technology, study it as a physical object. With various imaging techniques and machines, we can watch as different parts of the brain are more or less active; we can see how information flows around the brain, in the form of neurons firing and causing other neurons to fire. For example, we can observe deficits in patients with brain injuries in known places. During open-brain surgery on epileptics, surgeons have located areas in the left hemisphere corresponding to certain specific vocabulary items. As another example, brain imaging reveals a difference between the processing of significantly related senses of a word (e.g. *neck*, of a person or a bottle) and processing of accidentally homophonous words (e.g. *bank*, side of a river or financial institution). One more example is the detection of a signature pattern of electrical activity, a so-called N400 effect, when a person detects a clash of meanings in an anomalous sentence like *He buttered his toast with shoe-leather*. Such are small but promising steps in what might be called 'neurosemantics', the study of brain activity specifically related to the storage and processing of meanings.

Don't get too alarmed here—neuroscience is not yet in a position to describe the firings of neurons that may trigger someone saying *The car is around the corner*, let alone *I love you*. Nor could it ever in principle hope to find mental correlates of the whole meanings of those utterances, because some of the things referred to in them, the car, the 'I', and the 'you', exist outside the speaker's head. But inside the speaker's head, we assume, there must be some ideas, or some concepts, or some mental representations, call them what you like, of the things out in the world he is talking about, e.g. the car, the corner, or himself or his declared beloved. The things in the world that we talk about are our common point of reference when we communicate. Communication is only successful when both parties know from prior experience at least some of the things that are mentioned. If a guide book says *turn left at the gorse bush* (not a fictitious example!), and the reader has no concept of a gorse bush, communication has broken down.

The relationship between words and things, i.e. meaning, is indirect, mediated by concepts in the heads of language users. So we have three kinds of entity: linguistic entities, such as words and sentences; mental entities, such as concepts; and worldly objects and relations, such as dogs and clouds, and eating and being higher than. (We'll postpone for the moment consideration of non-physical entities such as God and the square root of minus one.) The mental entities, the concepts, face both ways, being the link between language and the world. In terms of the brain, we know that concepts are somehow stored there, but we have little idea of exactly how. I will assume that one aspect of meanings is certain brain states involved in triggering the production of utterances, even though we can't say in detail what they are. If you're uneasy about this, think of the nineteenth-century search for the source of the Nile. People knew the Nile must have a source, as all rivers do, and they knew it was somewhere in the middle of Africa. Eventually it was located. The phrase *the source of the Nile* was not a meaningless phrase just because no one had yet pinpointed its referent. Equally, the set of neural potentials, existing inside a particular brain circuitry, corresponding to my concept of a gorse bush, for example, does exist, as I systematically respond to the sight, scent, and feel of gorse bushes. Maybe you don't have that concept of a gorse bush, but you could acquire it, given some examples, and then you and I could talk about gorse bushes. Neuroscience will never get to the level of specificity of pinpointing a range of such esoteric concepts in the heads of particular individuals, not because it's in principle an impossible demand, but because it's not important enough as a research goal.

'What is the meaning of "meaning"?' is a hoary old question. It sounds dangerously circular. But when we carefully separate out the different ideas that are included in this cover-all term, it's not so problematic. Part of the meanings we convey in language are concepts. An evolutionary perspective starts from creatures who have concepts of parts of their world, but who as yet have no conventional ways of communicating these concepts to others (and perhaps no desire to do so, as discussed in the previous chapter). All higher non-human animals fit this description. Of extant species, only *Homo sapiens* has attached linguistic labels, words, to concepts. This acknowledges that some (but not all) aspects of what we mean by 'meaning' exist independently of communication between people, as in the simpler concepts by which animals manage their lives. What were the evolutionary predecessors of concepts before they got harnessed into the languages we speak?

Beyond here and now

The term 'concept' itself is a battleground. On the one hand, some, particularly some philosophers, deny that non-humans can ever have concepts. For them, a concept is essentially bound up with language; only creatures with language, so only humans, can have concepts. This view is now substantially eroded, and a majority of researchers are happy to talk about concepts in non-human animals. The evolutionary question of how humans got to be capable of having concepts is seldom posed. In this section I will start to trace an evolutionary path to full human concepts, through a stage that I label 'proto-concepts', to indicate that they form a basis for the later evolution of more human-like concepts. It is unlikely that proto-concepts, let alone fully human concepts, sprang into being fully fledged, with no antecedents visible in less cognitively developed species. Behaviours can be ordered along an evolutionary scale, from very simple reflexes, leading to what all are happy to recognize as indicating possession of full concepts, namely human concepts.

As a starting point, an essential, but not yet sufficient, criterion for possession of a concept is a systematic response to classes of things in the world. Simple reflex behaviours satisfy this criterion. A frog only jumps at objects of a certain size moving in a certain way, typically insects. A specific pattern of connections in the frog's brain responds to this class of stimuli and directly triggers the jumping response. For the frog, this class of events is in a limited way 'meaningful', using this term in its very general sense of 'significant'. Moving flies are significant in the life of frogs. At this point, using this broad sense of 'significant', we don't ask what the moving insect is significant *of* to the frog. The moving insect is not a symbol that stands for anything. But the frog's brain is organized to provide a coherent partitioning of its experiences into FLY and NON-FLY. Frogs certainly have richer lives than this, and males in the mating season, at least, can discriminate other frogs from non-frogs. Frogs and indeed all animals can occasionally be fooled, but their internal representations of significant classes of object out in the world are good enough to help them survive and mate. So here we have a plausible evolutionary starting point, internal mental representations of classes of objects, and probably of classes of events and states of affairs, at least in animals a bit less primitive than the frog.

Frogs' mental representations of flies do no work beyond provoking a jumping response. As far as we know, a frog's brain does not use its fly-related potential neuron firings to imagine flies when there are none around, or to plan its next fly-catching moves, or recall past delectable flies. There is a direct linkage between the perceptual mechanisms detecting fly-like objects and the motor mechanisms for catching them. The impulses go straight through from perception to motor response without stopping to register on any long-term memory. In this sense, the frog is far from having a full concept of flies. But the frog can form a temporary 'percept' of a fly, and the formation of percepts is a start on the evolutionary road to concepts.

I have used the metaphor of 'representations' freely, as is usual in this area. It is a potentially misleading term. It may, quite wrongly, conjure up an idea of the brain as like a gallery of pictures or sculptures that one can stroll among and inspect as objects. Pictures in a gallery are static, and made of the wrong stuff. There are no pictures or symbols in the head, let alone in the rest of the central nervous system, such as the spinal cord. The nervous system is a vast complex network of connected neurons, each with a different potential to transmit impulses to other neurons, triggered by different stimuli transmitted inward from the peripheral senses, and by the inputs received from other less peripheral neurons. This network is never at rest. There is always something going on in it, as in any living body. How, in such a constantly dynamic interconnected arrangement, can there be separate 'representations'? I will explain this special sense of 'representation', quite informally.

The first step is to realize that the neural network is not homogeneous. It is not the case that every neuron is equally connected to every other, with an equal propensity to respond to the sum of their inputs. The system has a skewed 'architecture'. There are many different types of neuron, with different specialisms. And the connections are severely channelled into pathways, just as main trunk roads in a country connect major hubs. Information gets concentrated at such hubs in the brain, and from them, information is transmitted outward in less focused ways, to a range of other targets. As a concrete example, consider visual inputs from the eyes. Through a number of intermediate stations, originally visual information, starting at the retinas, reaches the visual cortex at the back of the head. There it is reasonable to speak of representations being temporarily formed, in this case simple representations of boundaries between light and dark or motion of lines in parts of the visual field. This step is justified because there is a constant correlation between certain patterns of firing in the visual cortex and real light/dark boundaries or motion of lines out in the world seen by a subject. These representations of lines result from collation of inputs from both eyes. From the visual cortex, information flows to other places, including the temporal lobes, where known centres exist for the recognition of categories from the external world, such as colours or faces. At this point it is fair to speak of a representation being formed, say, of a particular colour or a particular face. More complex representations are roughly the sum (informally speaking) of other simpler representations, as representation of a whole face results from simpler representations, say of lines and colours. In a similar way, representations can be formed of particular categories of sound, of smell, taste, and so on. And there can be complex multimodal representations, resulting from inputs from different senses, such as vision and hearing. So far, all these are 'cued' representations, in the words of cognitive scientist Peter Gärdenfors. They are fleeting reactions to current input from the senses, though not so ephemeral as to have no effect on the animal's behaviour. It is in this sense that one can talk of a (cued) representation of, say, FLY in the brain of a frog.

Cued representations, the fleeting patterns of neural firings correlated with known categories of input from the world, differ from 'detached' representations (again Peter Gärdenfors' term). Cued representations depend for their existence on long-term potentials to fire in certain ways consistent with certain types of external input. While an animal is attending to something in the outside world, a pattern of activity is maintained in its brain. With shifts of attention, cued patterns of firing subside and give way to others, triggered by new focused information coming in through the senses. Now, in animals more complex than a frog, the patterns of firing associated with external categories of input can also be triggered in the absence of such input. The potential for a given pattern of firing to be triggered internally gives rise to a detached representation, because it can arise 'detached' in time from external stimuli. (Linguist Derek Bickerton has parallel terms, namely 'online thinking', in response to immediately present stimuli, versus 'offline thinking', for mental activity not triggered by an immediate external stimulus.) Languageless animals can have detached representations, so clearly some degree of detached mental representation or offline thought existed before language. I will go through some examples, starting from the most simple detached representations, not very far removed in time from the associated cued representations, up through a graded sequence of more and more detached representations.

Any animal that chases prey (not just grabbing it opportunistically as it passes, like a frog) will keep the prey in mind while the latter temporarily disappears up a tree or down a burrow. The predator can't see the prey, but it has it in mind. To 'have something in mind' is to have a representation of it in one's brain. In psychology, this is studied under the heading of 'object permanence'. Creatures with some sense of object permanence, from thousands of different species, keep in their minds an idea of something they have just seen disappear somewhere. The representation may decay over a few minutes or last at least as long as a day, in the case of chimpanzees. Panzee, a symbol-trained chimpanzee, could remember where a human had hidden some fruit a day before and signalled its whereabouts to another human. Of course humans can remember events for much longer, and they also remember a far wider class of events, not just involving food. This reflects humans' generally greater curiosity about the world, not directly related to survival or reproduction.

A perceived thing has a bundle of features that distinguish it from other things. While attending to a thing (which could be a person or another animal), its properties, such as its colour, shape, or size, are bound together by the fact that they all emanate from the same cuing location out in the world, where the thing is perceived to be. It is known from neuroscience that the tasks of attending to a location in the space around one and registering the properties coming in from that location are managed by two different brain mechanisms, respectively the 'dorsal stream' and the 'ventral stream'. These brain pathways work together seamlessly in healthy animals, human and non-human alike.

Many animals that live in groups can remember, and systematically respond to, a large number of other individuals in their group. They know who is a friend or ally, who is aggressive and needs to be avoided. This information is stored for long periods, often many years, usually in the absence of the individuals thus represented in the animal's mind. Baboons and elephants are among the species known to have these capabilities. They have detached representations of the things they remember. In this case, the binding together of the properties of the remembered object cannot be done by a stream of sensation from outside. Instead, any animal that remembers individual things in their absence must form an 'index', an internal pointer associated with all the properties of the remembered object, keeping it apart from other remembered objects, which may share some but not all of its properties. So even memory for individual things involves some structuring of what is in an animal's mind. The structure involves two different sorts of information: the index, and the properties bound to it. It has been argued that this mental combination of an index and properties is the basis for the most fundamental structure that logicians, quite independently, postulate between a logical predicate and its arguments. Since any animal that has long-term memory of objects has this degree of mental structuring, they share with humans at least this aspect of the form of logical thought. The terms 'index' or 'pointer' here are metaphorical, but apt. The idea is that what goes on in the brain when remembering an object and its properties is parallel to what happens in communicative language, where an object is identified by one part of a signal and described by other parts, as, for example, in *That's a cow*.

Experiments with birds and mammals show that many species not only remember individuals but also both remember past events and plan future moves. Memories of whole events are more complex than memories of individual objects, because several individuals at a time can participate in a perceived event. If you remember your mother passing your father a slice of turkey (say), that is a memory bringing together three objects (Mum, Dad, and the turkey slice), plus somehow binding them all together in an action categorized as PASSING. The next step in evolution toward full human-like concepts is a capacity to store, perhaps for only a short time, some memory of an experienced event, and act in response to that inner representation, without immediate stimulus from outside. A key idea here is that of 'episodic memory'.

Episodic memory is memory for events that have happened to one. People suffering from amnesia, often due to brain trauma, cannot recall what experiences they have been through, such as where they got up this morning, how they got to the police station, or episodes with their friends and relations. They have lost their episodic memory. They haven't lost all memory, as they can still speak fluently, knowing the meanings of words, and can sing songs and recite rote-learnt poetry. It was once claimed that only humans have episodic memory. Episodic memory for very distant events has been called 'mental time travel', and it is clear that only humans can remember details of things that have happened to them years before. But at smaller time frames, up to about a day, it is now evident that some non-human animals have episodic memory.

Scrub jays hide food and remember where they have hidden it, what type of food it was (perishable or non-perishable), and roughly how long ago they hid it. In controlled experimental conditions, give a scrub jay a maggot (perishable), let it hide it, and keep it away from the caching place for enough time for the maggot to decay. When released, the jay will not go to where it hid the maggot. Give the bird a nut (non-perishable) and keep it confined for the same amount of time before you release it, and the bird will go straight to where it hid the nut. In the cautious words of the researchers, psychologist Nicky Clayton and colleagues, scrub jays have 'episodic-like memory'. They remember the WHERE, the WHAT, and the WHEN of events significant to them.

Episodic memory for specific events in non-humans is quite short-lived, lasting no more than a day at most. This contrasts with their memory for particular individuals, usually from their own social group, which can persevere for many years in some species, such as elephants. This shows that objects (especially significant objects such as fellow group members) are more readily and more permanently remembered than events. Probably this is because objects are in some sense less complex than events, which involve the interaction of several objects.

Another piece of evidence that some non-human animals keep a representation in their brains of experienced events comes from studies of rats dreaming. Yes, that's right, rats dream, and neuroscientists Kenway Louie and Matthew Wilson have recorded their sequences of brain firings while in REM sleep. These rats had been trained to run mazes, and their brain activity was also recorded as they ran the mazes. There was a significant correlation between the brain patterns during the wakeful maze-running and the dreaming states. Some of these reiterated sequences of firings lasted for minutes. The best interpretation is that the rats are reliving their wakeful experiences while asleep—more, and different, evidence of episodic memory in non-humans.

While on the subject of rats' memories, another study makes a good connection between memory of past experiences and planning for future actions. Rats allowed to explore a maze with many arms looking for food were taken out for 15 minutes, before they had found the food. On being put back in the maze, they often started searching again where they had left off. Their accuracy in starting again at the 'right' place depended on either how many arms of the maze they had already searched or, conversely, how many arms were left to search. They were equally good if the number of arms searched in the past or remaining to be searched was quite low, and equally not so good if more arms had been searched or remained to be searched. Describing their results, psychologist Robert Cook and colleagues used the terms 'retrospective memory' for mental representations of past experience, and 'prospective memory' for representations used in planning future action. This shared representation of past and future applies to humans as well. But of course we and the rats have no trouble distinguishing past from future.

Going public with thoughts

With one notable exception, non-human animals do not communicate to each other about things away from the immediate time and place of the communication. The exception is honeybees. Scout honeybees find nectar, fly back to the hive, sometimes over more than a kilometre, and inform the bees in the hive of the direction and distance of the food. This system is completely innate, hardwired by the honeybee genes, and it relates to only one kind of message, the whereabouts of food (and potential nest sites). These social insects are so far removed from humans that it is not profitable to seek any antecedents to human communication in the behaviour, impressive though it is, of such tiny-brained creatures.

The exceptional honeybees forced us into a digression. Apart from them, all communication by non-human animals is about the here and now, never about things distant in time or place. A distinguishing feature of human language is that it allows displaced reference, i.e. mention of things not in the here and now, lacking in other (non-bee) animal communication. The existence of a degree of episodic memory in scrub jays, chimpanzees, rats, and other animals shows that this is not because the animals can only have concepts of things immediately present to them. Thus, an essential foundation for a feature of human language is present in many non-humans, namely an ability (admittedly limited) to entertain thoughts about things not immediately present. It's just that the non-human animals don't communicate to each other about such things.

Actually, the absence of displaced reference in other animal communication is only true from the viewpoint of the sender of a message. Chimpanzees and other apes and some monkeys send food calls when they find food—'Hey, tasty stuff over here'. The other animals receiving the signal are not at the place of the food referred to, so in this sense, the message is about something which is not where they, the hearers, are. But is this reference in the sense that the hearers of the food call actually bring to mind a (proto-)concept of food, rather than just reflexly moving in the direction of the call? The same question arises in the case of the vervet monkeys mentioned in the last chapter. When they make or hear alarm calls, are they really conjuring up a representation of the predator in the minds of their hearers? A view not ascribing this much complexity to the vervet monkeys would be that they have evolved to have reflex responses to the calls. In this view, they simply run up a tree when hearing a 'bark' call, without the idea of a leopard entering the monkey's mind, and simply dive under the bushes when hearing a 'chutter' call, without any idea of an eagle occurring to them.

Experiments with other monkeys with similar systematic alarm calls to the vervets suggest that this reflex hypothesis is wrong, and that monkeys do, for a brief time at least, entertain a representation of the relevant type of predator in their heads. These are experiments by psychologist Klaus Zuberbühler and his colleagues, carried out in the African tropical forest with Diana monkeys. The experimenters recorded four kinds of sound: two alarm calls and two noises made by predators, an eagle screech and a leopard growl. In one experimental condition, they played back to the monkeys in the forest first an alarm call, and five minutes later the noise made by the predator connected with that alarm call. For example, first they played back the eagle alarm call, and five minutes later gave playback of an eagle screeching—likewise for leopard call and leopard's growl. In the other experimental condition, the played-back calls and predator noises were not matched, so for instance, the monkeys first heard an alarm call for an eagle, and five minutes later they heard a leopard growling. In the condition where the second played-back sound matched the first played-back call, the monkeys showed significantly less alarm than when the second played-back noise did not match the alarm call they had heard five minutes earlier. This is consistent with the alarm call having evoked in the monkeys' minds a representation of the relevant predator type, so that when five minutes later they heard evidence of just that type of predator, they were not surprised. On the other hand, if you have heard a call bringing to mind one sort of predator, and then hear evidence of a different type of predator nearby, that is more of a surprise. In sum, the responses of some animals to calls by their conspecifics seem to be more than simple reflexes. The calls cause the receivers to form some representation in their minds of the relevant referent, e.g. of some type of predator or food, for a short while at least.

More abstract thinking

A kind of experiment with apes and monkeys shows interesting differences between species in their use, or non-use, of internal representations. These experiments, pioneered by psychologist Duane Rumbaugh, are called 'reversal learning' experiments. They work in two stages. First, an animal is trained to associate a reward with a given stimulus A, and no reward with a different stimulus B. Lots of animals can be trained in this way, with more or less effort. Now, in the second stage of the experiment, the same animal is trained on the exact reverse of the stimulus–response pairs of the first stage, associating a reward with stimulus B and no reward with stimulus A. This may seem a cruel thing to do, but it reveals an interesting fairly consistent difference between apes and monkeys. (We are more closely related to apes than to monkeys.) Monkeys, it seems, need painstakingly to unlearn what they learned in the first stage and then relearn for the second task. The better they have learned in the first stage, the more difficult is the unlearning and relearning.

In a way, this is not so surprising, but apes have a cleverer way of coping with this contradictory situation. For the apes, contrastingly, the more thoroughly they have learned the first task, the easier it is for them to learn the second task. What can we make of this? A simple proposal is that the apes are learning the second task by in some sense realizing, 'Aha, it's the opposite of what I learnt before'. That's an easy way to learn the new task, if you have the mental wherewithal to store a rule (from the first task) and then apply a reversing, or oppositeness, operation to the stored rule. The monkey/ape dichotomy is not perfect here, as one species of monkeys, capuchins, behaves somewhat more like apes. But the difference between animals who can learn the second task by applying an oppositeness operation to a rule and those who can't shows up an evolutionary progression toward mental representations and operations on them that are more human-like. What is going on in the heads of the relatively advanced animals is more than a simple reflex link between perception of the stimulus and a motor response.

The oppositeness operation apparently applied by apes in the reversal learning experiment involves an abstract relation, in the sense that no concrete object can have 'a property of oppositeness'. Oppositeness requires a comparison. Many animals of a wide variety of species have shown themselves capable of learning the similarly relational concepts of SAME and DIFFERENT. Animals as diverse as sea lions and parrots can be trained to judge whether two stimuli belong in the same class (SAME) or not (DIFFERENT). And many of them don't forget what they have learned. A California sea lion remembered the same/different patterns he had been trained on ten years afterwards. It is not at all surprising that animals can learn to make same/different judgements. Getting on in the world involves classifying somewhat dissimilar things into classes, so that all members of a class can be treated the same, if that works in the animal's life.

Some experimental animals have, however, really surprised us in the degree of abstractness they can mentally handle. Alex the African grey parrot, now sadly dead, trained by psychologist Irene Pepperberg, was a star performer. Alex could be shown a tray with three objects with one property in common (either its shape or its colour or its material) and asked, *What's same?* Conveniently, Alex was a talking parrot who had learned enough of the necessary English words. Most of the time he answered correctly (e.g. *Colour*), doing well better than chance. He could also be asked *What's different?* if the objects on the tray only differed in one property. He could even, if asked *What's same?*, and the objects on the tray had nothing in common, say *None*, most of the time correctly. Though these tasks are trivial for a human, they are not simple. Take the case where the objects had one property in common, say their blue colour, but had different shapes and were made of different material. Pondering the *What's same?* question, Alex would have needed to survey each object, remember its colour, its shape, and its material, and then mentally go over his list of these properties seeing which property belonged to all three objects. In our example case, this is the property BLUE. Now he can't answer *Blue*; his answer must be more abstract, and involve the second-order judgement that blue is a colour, and he duly answers *Colour*. Logically, the concept BLUE is a first-order property, the simplest kind, belonging directly to physical objects. The judgement that a range of such first-order properties, BLUE, RED, YELLOW, BLACK, and WHITE, come under the higher concept COLOUR, whereas SQUARE, ROUND, TRIANGULAR, and FLAT belong to a different higher concept, SHAPE, clearly shows command of a degree of abstraction. There was enough control over the training and testing regimes to ensure that Alex was genuinely generalizing over such abstractions, and not just rote-memorizing a list of correct answers for each possible experimental combination of circumstances. It is likely that Alex was only able to manage this degree of abstraction because he had been taught concrete terms including *red, blue, square,* and *round.* He used the concrete terms as props in his thinking out of the more abstract answers. We will see further examples of the ways in which words actually enable thought in Chapter 6.

So a wide range of animals have mental representations of things and events that are significant to them, and they can put these mental representations to use in internal calculations, such as in planning future actions and learning new tasks. It's not unreasonable to call these 'proto-concepts' at least, if you still want to deny non-humans possession of full concepts. Many non-human animals have quite richly structured information in their heads about the world around them. Only humans have developed rich systems for externalizing this information in the form of public messages. We will begin to see how in the next chapters.

5

We began to speak, and to hear differently

In the previous chapter we saw how non-human animals already possess fairly complex mental representations of the world. In the chapter before that we saw the foundations of the motivation to communicate, in factors such as mind-reading, trust, and cooperation. A species that develops these properties, then, has both something to communicate and a motivation to communicate it. What is lacking in the story so far is the physical wherewithal to implement the communication. In this chapter, I will focus on the origins of the physical apparatus of speech, as the dominant medium of human communication.

Speaking is one of our most complex motor activities. In its speed of execution and the number of separate articulators, it is a skill comparable to a virtuoso performance by a concert pianist. Yet healthy people do it all the time casually and with virtually no effort. Our vocal tract anatomy, i.e. the shape, relative positions, and connections between the parts, has evolved substantially since our last common ancestor with the other apes. 'Exaptation' is a term used to describe an evolutionary functional shift whereby a trait serving one purpose evolves out of a trait serving another function. The evolution of birds' feathers from reptilian scales is an example often given, as is the evolution of wings for flight from appendages used for temperature regulation. All parts of the human vocal tract are exapted and originally served functions other than speech, in particular eating and breathing, and still do. The vocal tract is not static; modifications of the shape produce the range of sounds we find in the world's languages. The degree of fine voluntary control over this shape-shifting 'organ' has also evolved, so that we can play this instrument with great precision and delicacy. Data relevant to the evolution of the vocal tract comes from a little fossil evidence and from comparisons among modern humans, other apes and some other animals whose performance has surprised us. I will start with the comparative anatomical evidence. We'll tour the principal parts of the human vocal tract, emphasizing differences between them and those of other apes. This comparative physiological approach is the best we can do, as vocal tracts leave no fossils (though some relevant evidence can be gleaned from fossils—see later).

Human and non-human vocal anatomy

The larynx, or 'Adam's apple', sits on top of the trachea (windpipe) and houses the vocal cords, whose vibration produces the basic buzz of the voice. The acoustic effect of this buzz is moderated by the shape of the chambers above it, through which the airstream from the lungs passes, eventually out past the lips or through the nose. The remarkable thing about the position of the human larynx, after about 2 years of age, is that it is low in the throat, compared to its position in other primates. The typical primate larynx is up close to the back of the mouth, near where the nasal passage and the oral passage join. In humans, the lower position of the larynx allows a hollow space, the pharynx, up between it and the back of the mouth. If you point with your fingers sideways, inwards and upwards at about 45° just below your chin and above the Adam's apple, you are pointing at your pharynx. The pharynx provides an extra shape-shiftable chamber through which passes the air carrying the vocal buzz. Thus the human vocal tract, above the larynx, has an 'upside-down L' shape, with an approximate right-angle bend between the vertical pharynx and the horizontal mouth cavity. Because of the versatility of the tongue, the pharynx can be narrowed by pulling the tongue root backward, which lowers the body of the tongue in the mouth, widening the oral cavity. Conversely, the tongue body can be pushed high in the mouth, narrowing the oral cavity and widening the pharyngeal cavity. Thus, the airflow from the lungs can pass either through a narrow cavity first, then into the next and wider oral chamber, or through a wider cavity first and then through a narrowed oral chamber. This design is a 'double resonator system'. It's actually more complicated than I have described, because the tongue can shape-shift in different ways, the lips can be protruded or retracted, and the nasal passage can be opened or closed off by the velum, creating a wide range of different-shaped passages for the flow of air. When the vocal cords are vibrating, the relative shape and narrowness of the vertical and horizontal cavities are the most significant determinants of the different vowel sounds that humans can make.

There is a correlation between the shape of the mouth and pharynx when making vowel sounds and certain acoustic qualities of the waveform produced. The vocal cords vibrate, and as the waves produced pass upward through the vocal tract, resonances at some frequencies are damped out and others are made relatively prominent. The distribution of these resonances can be shown in a spectrogram. A spectrogram of a sound is a graph plotting time along the bottom axis against frequencies, in cycles per second (Hertz, Hz), on the vertical axis. For vowels, the frequencies of the more prominent resonances show up as dark bands in a spectrogram. The frequencies thus picked out are called 'formants'. There are many such dark bands, or formants, but the two or three at the lowest frequencies are most crucial to identifying particular vowels. Each different vowel has its own profile of formants, its distinctive bands of energy. For a typical male speaker, an [i] vowel as in Scottish English *pea*, for example, has a first formant ('F1') at about 300 Hz, and a second formant ('F2') at about 2,500 Hz. Thus the formant pattern for this vowel has first and second formants (F1, F2) well separated, and acoustically the vowel is called 'diffuse'. By contrast an [ɑ] vowel, as in London English *father*, has its first and second formants very close together slightly below and slightly above 1,000 Hz. Thus this vowel is labelled as acoustically 'compact'. 'High front' vowels articulated with the body of the tongue in a high front position, like [i], are acoustically diffuse; articularly low back vowels like [ɑ] are acoustically compact. A high back vowel, [u] as in French *vous* or German *Du*, has its F1 at about 310 Hz, and F2 around 800 Hz. For typical female speakers these formant levels, especially those of F2, are higher by between 10% and 30%, and the male/female differences are somewhat different across languages. Note that none of the above values are for fundamental frequency ('F0'), the musical pitch on which the vowel may be sung. Any vowel sound made by the human vocal tract, including many intermediate ones that I have not illustrated, has a particular pattern of acoustic formants. All of this acoustic diversity in vowels is made possible by the flexibility of the L-shaped chamber above the larynx. Because their larynxes are so relatively high up, other primates cannot produce the range of different vowels that humans can make, and which are so crucial in conveying meaning.

In the evolution of the human vocal tract since the split with other apes, the adult larynx descended to its lower position. Phonetician Philip Lieberman has persuasively argued that the ultimate cause of the human lowered larynx is its function in producing different vowels. This is a case of natural selection for more effective communication. The lowered larynx actually brings with it a slightly greater risk of choking on food, as if the larynx is not carefully covered during swallowing, food can go down the wrong pipe, the trachea (windpipe) instead of the oesophagus (foodpipe). The evolutionary pressure to communicate outweighed the risk of choking.

Babies are born with their larynxes in a high position, like monkeys. This is functional, as there is a reduced risk of choking, and babies are not yet talking. A baby can suckle and breathe at the same time. Milk taken in through the mouth can be kept separate from air taken through the nose, because the baby's larynx at this stage connects more directly to the nasal passage. (Don't try sucking a drink through a straw down into your tummy while breathing in through your nose at the same time.) By about the end of the first year, the human larynx descends to its near-adult lowered position. This is a case of ontogeny recapitulating phylogeny, the growth of the individual reflecting the evolution of the species. Of course, it is not necessary for ontogeny to recapitulate phylogeny, but it often happens, and makes child development one strand of plausible, though not compelling, evidence for particular evolutionary pathways.

Primatologist Takeshi Nishimura and his team have shown that there is some lowering of the larynx during the infancy of chimpanzees, although not so much as to make the double-resonator vocal tract characteristic of human adults. They suggest that the evolutionary descent of the human larynx actually happened in two stages. The first descent, observable in both human and chimpanzee infants, involves the body of the larynx descending relative to the position of the hyoid bone. The hyoid bone is a horseshoe-shaped bone in the throat above the larynx and behind the root of the tongue. The hyoid is connected downwards by muscles to the larynx, and upwards to the tongue and floor of the mouth by other muscles. The second descent of the larynx, which only happened in humans, was the further descent of the hyoid bone itself, with the larynx still a constant distance below it, to a position much lower than seen in other apes. These researchers suggest that it was only the second descent that was functionally motivated by pressure for more differentiated speech. A two-stage evolutionary process shows a more gradual, less abrupt transition from the basic primate design to the human shape. In this view the first descent of the larynx (with the hyoid staying high) was a preadaptive step which happened to make the second, characteristically human, step viable. The overall picture suggested is of a route to human form initiated, but not completed, even before the chimpanzee/human split about 6 million years ago.

Psychologist Tecumseh Fitch has shown that several non-human species have larynxes lowered during vocalization. X-ray film of dogs barking shows a fast lowering of the larynx during the bark, after which the larynx returns to its high position. Male deer also lower their larynxes prominently while roaring; one can plainly see the Adam's apple in the throat moving downward during a roar. The resting position of the deer larynx is not as high up behind the velum as in monkeys. In neither deer nor dogs does the lowering of the larynx during the vocalization contribute significantly to any change of acoustic formant pattern. You don't hear a change in 'vowel quality' as in a human diphthong during a dog's bark or a deer's roar, though there is often a change in fundamental pitch. In both dogs and deer the sound from the vibrating cords passes through a much straighter tract than the human L-shaped tract. Chimpanzees are, not surprisingly, slightly closer to humans in the range of vowel-like sounds they can make. Although their vocal tract does not have the marked right-angle bend seen in humans, there is a slight curvature, and natural chimpanzee calls, especially the so-called 'pant-hoot', can be heard by a willing human hearer as having sounds something like human [ɑ] and [u]. But chimpanzees cannot make sounds anything like human high front vowels [i] and [e]. (We will see the significance of this high front region of the vowel space again later.)

Koalas, very unusually, have permanently lowered larynxes, so the human larynx position is not absolutely unique. But the L-shape of the human vocal tract, enabling us to make vowels of different vowel qualities, is unique. Fitch has suggested that size exaggeration in mating calls is an evolutionary motivator for larynx lowering. A lower larynx while vocalizing gives an impression of a larger animal. In human males, there is a second, slight, lowering of the larynx at puberty (the 'breaking of the voice'), and this may have a size exaggeration function for sexual attraction. The first lowering of the larynx, occurring in both males and females at a very young age, is not plausibly attributed to a size exaggeration function, but is an evolutionary development allowing greater versatility in making vowel sounds of different qualities, as Philip Lieberman had argued.

Some curious facts suggest that the story is more complicated. Some animals with vocal tracts very different from humans can make sounds not unlike distinct human vowels. An amusing case involves Hoover, a harbour seal adopted by a Maine fisherman. Hoover made a muffled but passable imitation of his adoptive human parent saying, in a Maine accent even, *get over here* and *hurry*. Seals have vocal tracts quite different from humans, but something human-vowel-like was possible for Hoover. Recently, whistles of a beluga whale have been claimed to be imitative of human speech, as have the honkings of a Korean zoo elephant. People sometimes lean over backwards to see human traits where few exist, as when we see a man's face in the full moon. (There is no suggestion that the seal, the whale, or the elephant know anything of the meanings of the utterances they creakily imitate.) In the context of debate about the human lowered larynx, the most perplexing case of animals imitating human speech is that of 'talking birds'. Parrots passably imitate human speech, with many distinct vowels. Birds don't use their larynxes for sound-making. At the heart of the avian vocal apparatus is a syrinx, an organ quite unlike the mammalian larynx. Some experiments suggest that a parrot makes different speech-like sounds by moving its tongue to modify the shape of the passage that air flows through. In this basic respect, parrot speech works the same way as human speech, with a sound source, the larynx or syrinx, surmounted by an airway of changeable shape acting as a filter on the sound. The chirps and screeches made by parrots in the wild are not at all like human speech, and their imitative abilities only come out in captivity. There are several cases of animals having a capacity for rudiments of human behaviour that only surfaces in captivity (as we have seen in other chapters).

As early as the 1970s Philip Lieberman had argued, based on indirect extrapolations from human babies, chimpanzees, and Neanderthal skeletons, that the larynx in Neanderthals could not have been in the descended position of the modern human larynx, and therefore Neanderthals were not able to articulate the same range of vowels as us. Few are convinced of this conclusion today. We will see some reasons for this scepticism just below.

Fossils

A terminological note: there are two kinds of 'fossil' (literally a thing dug up): preserved hard body parts such as bones and teeth, and imprints or casts of soft tissue that has rotted away, leaving a space to be filled by hardening minerals leaking in. The soft-tissue parts of the vocal tract, including tongues, lips, soft palates, and larynxes, decay in the ground, and no mineralized imprints of them have been found. So a lot that we would like to know about is missing from the fossil record. All the fossil evidence is from preserved bony parts. Bones can show marks of muscle attachments, and the direction in which the muscles pulled, but a lot of speculative extrapolation is involved in theorizing about the attached soft tissues. I'll mention three areas where fossils have been invoked: the hyoid bone, the thoracic canal, and the hypoglossal canals.

The larynx must be somewhat below the hyoid bone, but exactly how far is not a fixed proportion across species. As we have seen, the chimpanzee hyoid and larynx are rather close together, whereas the human hyoid and larynx are more distant from each other. Unfortunately, all that remains of fossil hyoid bones is their shape, and not their position, because none of the muscles have been preserved. So a fossilized hyoid bone in itself tells us nothing certain about the position of the larynx. In 1983, a nearly complete Neanderthal skeleton, including a hyoid bone, was discovered in Kebara cave, Israel, dating to 60,000 years ago. Later, another well-preserved Neanderthal hyoid bone was found at El Sidrón cave in Spain, dating to about 43,000 years ago. These Neanderthal hyoids were practically identical in size and shape to modern human hyoids, with faint signs of attachment to muscles. While the size and shape in themselves do not prove anything conclusive about the position of the Neanderthal larynx, the lack of any significant difference between the hyoids of the two species may indicate that it is more likely than not that other aspects of their vocal tracts were also very similar. On the other hand, the lower jaw of the Kebara specimen was markedly bigger and more robust than a modern human jaw, so the anatomical setting of the vocal tract was somewhat dissimilar.

Other research invoking the hyoid bone compares its shape in humans with its shape in other great apes. In the other apes, the hyoid bone has a spoon-bowl-shaped extension pointing outward from the middle of its U-shape. This extension is the 'hyoid bulla'. Gorillas, chimpanzees, bonobos, and orang-utans all have a bulla on their hyoid. The human hyoid has no bulla. It is more likely that our species lost its bulla than that the other apes independently gained one during their evolution. Interestingly, all these other apes also have 'air sacs', baggy structures attached to their vocal tract just above the vocal cords, and close to the hyoid. These sacs can be very big, with a capacity as much as two litres in some cases. If you imagine the vocal tract as a tunnel from the vocal cords outward through the mouth, the air sacs are like a large chamber off to the side of this tunnel. Any sound reverberating through the tunnel will be modified by extra resonances of air passing over the entrance to the sacs and eddying in and out of them. Phonetician Bart de Boer has made physical models of the human double-resonator vocal tract with and without the addition of this extra side chamber. The vowels synthesized through these models are less easily distinguished from each other by human judges if there is an extra chamber, modelling air sacs, than if there is not. The conclusion is that air sacs have an effect of muddying contrasts between vowels (though not obliterating them altogether). It is hypothesized that the loss of air sacs in the specifically human lineage was motivated by the more effective function of a sac-less vocal tract in making distinct vowel sounds. A few fossils allow us a peek at the possible timing of the loss of a hyoid bulla in the human lineage. An Australopithecine skeleton from about 3.3 million years ago has a well-preserved hyoid bone with the features of African ape hyoids, including a pronounced bulla. The El Sidrón and Kebara Neanderthal hyoids from 43,000 and 60,000 years ago are just like a modern human hyoid, with no bulla. In the 1990s two hyoid bones from *Homo heidelbergensis* were discovered in Spain, dating from about 600,000 years ago, and these also were shaped like modern human hyoids. The implication is that the human vocal tract had evolved to something like its modern shape already in *Homo heidelbergensis*, over half a million years ago.

Add to these discoveries the fact that, as mentioned in Chapter 1, Neanderthals had a modern human variant of FOXP2, a gene closely involved in the articulation of speech, and again it seems more likely than not, on the thin evidence, that Neanderthals, by 60,000 years ago, had a speech capability something like ours, though probably not identical. Further research, reviewed later in this chapter, accumulates to suggest the relative modernity of the speech capacities of Neanderthals, and possibly of their immediate ancestors, *Homo heidelbergensis*, though this is less well supported. None of this says anything directly about the grammatical abilities of pre-humans, of course.

Other fossil evidence for the origins of modern speech capacity comes from relics of the thoracic vertebral canal in Australopithecines and Neanderthals, compared with modern humans. This canal is a series of holes in successive vertebrae, lined up vertically and forming a conduit for the spinal cord containing nerves from the brain to the chest muscles. The spinal cord relays information significant in the control of breathing, alongside many other motor functions of the lower body.

Human breathing is remarkably controlled. While in other animals in-breaths and out-breaths are of roughly the same duration, human breathing while speaking is about 90% exhalation, with only about 10% of time saved for quick in-breaths. The exhalation itself is finely controlled, with a thin flow of air maintained at speeds and volumes conducive to vibrating the vocal cords as desired and yielding the appropriate pressure for plosive and fricative consonants, all while producing subtle intonation patterns. Other mammals have no such fine control over their breathing, even when vocalizing. A comparison of the 'laughter' of chimpanzees with human laughter is instructive. This type of chimpanzee vocalization is auditorily like human laughter, and may be justifiably called laughter because the animals do it during rough-and-tumble, apparently enjoyable, play. Chimpanzee laughter, like human laughter, is a series of short rather breathy syllables, but produced on alternating in- and out-breaths, quite like the 'Hee-haw' braying of a donkey, but with shorter syllables. Chimp laughter has been likened to the sound of sawing wood, with its quick back-and-forth strokes. But human laughter is all produced on an extended out-breath, just like our speech. Our adaptation to control of our exhalation has extended even to such spontaneous sounds as laughter.

The fossil evidence for relatively recent evolution of fine control of breathing comes from measurements of the minimal cross-sectional area of the spinal (or vertebral) canal. Biologists Anne McLarnon and Gwen Hewitt compared canal sizes, adjusted against overall body size, of over fifty specimens from a wide variety of non-human primates, two Australopithecine specimens, one *Homo erectus*, four Neanderthals, an early *Homo sapiens*, and seven fully modern humans. The results show a significant increase in relative canal size just in Neanderthals and *Homo sapiens*. The Australopithecines and *Homo erectus* pattern with the non-human primates. They attribute this difference to fine breath control in Neanderthals and modern humans, lacking in earlier species. The reasoning assumes that a larger aperture houses a greater number of nerves used for sending messages to the various chest muscles used in breath modulation. Although the nerves in the spinal cord are also used for regulating bipedal walking, bipedalism itself cannot be the main cause of the size difference, as Australopithecines and *Homo erectus* were also bipedal.

A less direct connection between fine breath control and bipedalism is likely, however. In animals who move about quadrupedally, the rhythm of breathing is closely linked with the rhythm of walking and running. In running, in particular, a chest firmly braced against the impact of the forelimbs with the ground is more effective than a chest with uncoordinated firmness and fullness of air. When walking, humans do not maintain any close coordination between their paces and their breathing. Indeed, we can easily talk in long sentences while walking. Even in running, while there tends to be some constant relation between pacing and breathing, it is not the one-pace-to-one-breath relationship typical of quadrupedal walkers. So it is possible that the earlier bipeds, perhaps even from Australopithecines onward, evolved away from a strict one-to-one relationship between their breathing and their walking, and that this was a preadaptive platform on which the later evolution of fine breath control in humans and Neanderthals could build. It is a nice example of relaxation of constraints paving the way for previously inaccessible evolutionary developments. Finally on the subject of breath control, note that you only need such fine control of exhalation in communication if you are producing rather long signals, presumably for somewhat complex messages, suggesting some indirect connection between human breath control and complex syntax.

You will have noted the speculative nature of extrapolating the era in which some modern speech capacity arose from the sizes of bony canals in fossils. So far, McLarnon and Hewitt's conclusions based on the vertebral canal have been accepted. But a similar study making inferences from fossil canal sizes to the emergence of modern speech abilities shows how fragile such arguments can be. In this case, the canals in question are the hypoglossal canals, little holes in the base of the skull, left and right, through which pass the hypoglossal nerves controlling tongue movement. Humans have uniquely complex control over the shape and movement of their tongues. Instructions for these delicate movements pass along the hypoglossal nerves through the hypoglossal canals. A rare case of unilateral (right side) damage to one of the hypoglossal nerves involved slurred speech, atrophy of the right side of the tongue, and deviation of the tongue, toward the right. This is instructive, illustrating the importance of this nerve for controlling the fine movements of the tongue during speech. It is a fair guess that the size of the hypoglossal canals is indicative of the degree of control an animal has over its tongue muscles. This was the reasoning of biological anthropologist Richard Kay and his colleagues. They measured the hypoglossal canals of some modern apes, some Australopithecines, *Homo habilis*, some Neanderthals, early humans, and modern humans. In their sample, they found a significant difference between the Australopithecines and non-human apes on the one hand and the Neanderthals and humans on the other hand. They concluded that fine control of the tongue for articulated speech appeared at least 400,000 years ago, probably with *Homo erectus*. Unfortunately, within a year, this conclusion was refuted by palaeoanthropologist David DeGusta and his team. They measured the hypoglossal canals of other non-human primates and Australopithecines, and found them to be within the modern human range. These researchers also found no correlation between the size of the hypoglossal canal and the number of nerve axons passing through it. These results demolish the earlier conclusions from the hypoglossal canal, and should make us more cautious in extrapolating modern abilities from fossils. I don't deny that it can be done, but at present the evidence is shaky. Humans at some stage developed far finer control over tongue movements than chimpanzees, who cannot produce anything passable as human consonants; but dating the emergence of this fine control has so far eluded us.

New animal data and new fossils keep turning up, and ingenious researchers continue to try to draw conclusions about the vocal abilities of our ancestors. What little evidence we have as of 2013 points weakly, I believe, to a conclusion that late Neanderthals at least and their *Homo sapiens* contemporaries had vocal tracts and fine control over them quite similar to modern humans, with the beginnings of these developments rooted earlier, probably in *Homo erectus*. But admittedly the evidence for this, or any alternative conclusion, is thin.

Questions about hearing speech

Humans have complementary abilities to produce and to perceive and interpret speech sounds. Today in communication these abilities work together. The range of sounds that we produce with our mouths and throats for communicative speech lies within the range of sounds that the human ear can detect. (Otherwise, what would be the use of speaking?) Speech and human hearing appear 'made for each other'. The evolutionary question that arises is: 'Which adapted to which?' During our evolution, did vocal tracts change their shape, and did the controlling motor mechanisms change, so that the sounds they could produce were specially fitted to what the pre-existing human ear could detect and disentangle into meaningful messages? This would be a one-way process of speech production adapting to our hearing, without the hearing itself becoming more specialized. The reverse one-way possibility is that human hearing adapted specifically to detect and interpret a new class of sounds—those which happened to be makeable by our vocal tracts as they already were. It's clear that speech sounds are not the only sounds we can hear. We (fortunately) can hear non-speech sounds, like rushing wind, footsteps, and thunder, but only a few gifted entertainers can make sounds approaching these with their vocal tracts. So on the face of things, it would appear that human hearing is general purpose, and not specifically adapted to speech.

These two hypothetical alternative one-way adaptive stories—either speech adapted to hearing or human hearing adapted to speech—are simple. A more complex story is that speech and human hearing co-evolved to some extent. Co-evolution of coordinating systems is common in complex organisms. In a co-evolutionary story about speech, human hearing, though admittedly versatile, has nevertheless become at least somewhat specialized for speech, and speech production has also evolved in ways specially suited to human hearing. In the previous two sections, we looked at our speech organs themselves, and the motor abilities for using them, with a view to tracing their evolutionary history. Now we'll consider the extent to which human hearing is special, compared to that of other animals.

When a normal adult human hears speech, a train of events occurs, penetrating further and further into the head from the out-side. The early processes are mechanical, and the later processes are neurological or 'electrical'. The mechanical processes are sensory, from vibrations picked up at the eardrum to the twitching of little hairs in the cochlea of the inner ear. After that, the processes are per-ceptual, a matter of how the brain interprets the information deliv-ered to it by the sensory system. Without sensation, there can be no perception. If certain key properties of a stimulus cannot be sensed, perception is hampered in analysing it. But often, with complex stim-uli as occur in nature, perception is robust enough to work around the lack of some input from the sensory system and successfully recognize a stimulus. Expectations due to context help. This makes it difficult to distinguish experimentally with realistic stimuli between an animal's raw sensory acuity and its perceptual abilities. In the interpretation of speech, we should also draw a line between speech perception, i.e. the delivery of phonological units such as phonemes, tones, rhythm, and intonation patterns, and subsequent lexical and grammatical processing which interprets the input as words and decodes sequences of words into their meanings. Here we are only concerned with auditory sensation and speech perception. We'll ask first whether raw human sound sensation (up to the cochlea) is interestingly different from that of related animals (answer: Yes). We will ask to what extent sensory differences between humans and non-humans may make perceptual processing of a speech signal into phonological units more difficult for other species. Next, we'll ask whether the phonological processing capacities of other species, even with adequate sensory input, are more limited than in humans. And finally, we will ask if humans process speech input any differently from other environmental noise. These are subtle questions.

Sensing sounds

The anatomy of our ear is broadly similar to that of closely related mammals. The sensory parts of mammal hearing systems have the same basic arrangements of outer, middle, and inner ear. The main business of converting acoustic waves to information for the brain happens in the middle and inner ear. Here all mammals have the same parts, in the same relation to each other, though varying in size and shape. Pressure waves in the air (i.e. sound) make the eardrum vibrate. From the eardrum to the cochlea, all mammals have the three ossicles (little bones), the malleus, incus, and stapes, bumping against each other in a chain, passing the vibrations on in moderated form. (The deep evolutionary history of the ossicles is interesting in itself, as two of them are exapted from reptile jawbones, and were originally not part of a hearing system at all.) In the labyrinth of the inner ear, the cochlea is a complex spiral structure with thousands of tiny hairs which respond to different frequencies in the incoming vibrations. After that point, the information transmitted to the brain is no longer acoustic but electrical, passing through auditory neurons.

Harmonic sounds, like the ring of a bell or a plucked guitar string, are relatively simple, having a fundamental frequency, the basic pitch of the note we hear, and sympathetic vibrations spaced at arithmetically defined intervals higher in the frequency range, the higher harmonics. More complex sounds, such as those made by consonants in speech, involve vibrations at many different frequencies, not spaced out in the neatly arithmetical way of higher harmonics. The hairs in the cochlea respond individually to different sound frequencies, so that the total pattern of information they pass on is a complex profile of the frequencies of the incoming sound. This much all mammal hearing has in common.

Mammals not closely related to humans can hear sounds at frequencies outside the human hearing range. Bats are the obvious example. Dogs also can hear more high-pitched sounds than humans. At the other end of the scale, elephants make deep rumblings, some just audible to humans and some so low-pitched as to be inaudible to humans. Mostly, the medium through which the vibrations pass is the ground, and the elephants detect these signals partly through their feet and trunks. Some of the sensations thus detected are passed through bone to the elephants' ears.

The raw hearing acuity of any species can be measured using pure tones, electronic beeps consisting of only a fundamental frequency. The acuity itself can be represented as an area on a two-dimensional plot of frequency against loudness. If you take a standard hearing test, this is the graph that the audiologist makes. Frequency is reckoned in cycles per second (Hertz, Hz), and the relevant measure of loudness is in decibels (dB) on a scale conventionally anchored to the threshold of human hearing at the frequencies where it is most sensitive, namely between 2,000 and 4,000 Hz. At this sweet spot between 2,000 and 4,000 Hz the typical young adult human ear can detect sounds down to a quietness said to be at zero decibels (0 dB). (So 'zero decibels' does not mean total absence of sound, contrary to popular metaphor.) The decibel scale is logarithmic to a base of 10; thus a tone at 10 dB is 10 times more intense than one at 0 dB, a tone at 20 dB is 100 times more intense, and one at 40 dB is 10,000 more intense (louder). The upper limit of normal acuity in loudness is where sound is so intense that it is painful and can cause damage to the ear, starting at about 85 dB in humans. The upper limit of acuity for frequency, at non-damaging loudness, is about 20,000 Hz, but, to be heard, sounds at this frequency need to be louder than sounds at the best frequencies around 3,000 Hz. At the lower limit, too, around

20 Hz, sounds need to be louder than those in that sweet spot to be heard. The range of fundamental frequencies producible by the normal human voice, from a basso low C at about 65 Hz to a soprano high C at just over 1,000 Hz, is well within this hearing range—no surprises there.

Pure tones as used in experiments on raw hearing acuity do not occur in nature. Complex sounds, as found in nature, have frequencies at many different levels. All of the frequencies in complex sound are in principle detectable, subject to the thresholds and upper limits, for loudness and frequency, of the species concerned. As we saw earlier, acoustic energy at higher frequencies than the basic buzz of the voice (the fundamental frequency) is important for recognizing different speech sounds. The first formant (F1) for the [i] vowel as in Scottish English *pea* is at about 300 Hz, and the second (F2) is at about 2,500 Hz. So we need to ask about particular sensitivities within the hearing range. Is human sound sensation different from that of closely related species in being specifically adapted to a range of frequencies that are important for recognizing speech sounds?

Chimpanzee hearing acuity differs from that of humans in interesting ways. In contrast to humans, chimpanzees have less auditory sensitivity to tones in the human 'sweet spot' range between 2,000 and 4,000 Hz than at both lower (1,000 Hz) and higher (8,000 Hz) frequencies. Where the graph of human sensitivity is U-shaped, the corresponding chimpanzee graph is complex and roughly ω-shaped. (On interpreting these U and ω letters, lower on the page is more sensitive, so humans have one most sensitive area in the graph at their sweet spot, while chimpanzees have two sweet spots and a 'sour', relatively less sensitive area between them.) The dip in chimpanzee acuity in the mid-range should not affect their ability to recognize most English vowels, whose first and second formants are below that mid-range. Primatologist Shozo Kojima has tested chimpanzee recognition of Japanese and French vowels and found that their reaction times in recognition tasks are slower than humans, although they did succeed at levels above chance in recognizing the vowels. This could be due to the unnaturalness of the task for a chimpanzee and the animal's relative lack of experience in recognizing speech sounds. Humans are very habituated to it, of course. But two vowels in particular were more problematic for chimpanzees, and these were [i] and [e], high front vowels and the only ones with an F2 above 2,000 Hz. So it is quite likely that at least some of the human skill in recognizing distinct vowels rests on a detailed difference in raw acuity compared to the most closely related ape.

Sound is transmitted through the ossicles to the cochlea, and some information is lost in this transmission. It has been suggested that the dip in chimpanzee acuity between 2,000 and 4,000 Hz can be attributed to the pattern of power transmission through these little bones. Accepting this, it is then possible to make estimates of hearing acuity across the frequency range based on the shapes and sizes of the ossicles. And here is a link to evolution. Palaeontologist Ignacio Martínez and his team have measured ossicles and the relevant parts of crania in *Homo heidelbergensis* skeletons and extrapolated a power transmission pattern similar to that in modern humans, and unlike that in chimpanzees, particularly in the 4,000 Hz region. They suggest that these individuals, who lived at least 350,000 years ago and were the probable ancestors of Neanderthals, already had a modern human-like hearing acuity function, presumably inherited from the common ancestor with humans, who lived earlier, at least 500,000 years ago. I am sceptical of how much can reasonably be extrapolated from a few fossil ossicles and crania. But the chimp/human differences in raw hearing acuity are not in doubt.

Somewhere in our descent from the common ancestor with chimpanzees, we developed acuity in the 2,000–4,000 Hz range that we did not have before. This change in acuity is not absolutely crucial to speech recognition, but it helps. People with impaired hearing in the middle frequencies show the same patterns of vowel recognition as chimpanzees. The evolution of greater sensitivity in the middle range could be the result of fine tuning by natural selection adapting human hearing to a corner (the high front vowels) of the acoustic space afforded by the vocal tract. But fine tuning is all it could be. Chimpanzees and bonobos manage pretty well at recognizing human speech, as attested by several symbol-trained animals. Panzee, a chimpanzee accustomed to hearing human speech in her day-to-day life, and associating spoken words with symbols on a lexigram board, could even manage at well above chance levels on systematically distorted speech, as psychologist Lisa Heimbauer and her team discovered. For technical reasons, Heimbauer's team did not conduct statistical tests on differences between humans and Panzee on this task, but their diagrams show a superior performance by humans. And their research did not single out any particular vowels (or consonants) on which Panzee had particular difficulty.

Kojima's team also found that chimpanzees can discriminate French and Japanese consonants quite well, apparently using the same acoustic cues as humans, but not performing as well. So, yes, chimpanzees have enough auditory sensitivity to recognize speech, but not as well as humans, and some of their deficits relate specifically to high front vowels. The hearing of the common ancestor of chimpanzees and humans would presumably have been about as well suited to human speech as modern chimpanzees, i.e. quite well, but not perfectly. In sum, we have here evidence for substantial continuity between other apes and ourselves, but also evidence of a degree of human specialness.

In the next two sections, we will examine a claim that 'speech is special'. Immediately, we must carefully separate two senses of this slogan. Many primate species have separate neural mechanisms for processing the calls of their conspecifics, as opposed to other environmental sounds, like wind rushing or falling trees. When, for example, a macaque hears another macaque's cry, specialized brain circuits in its left hemisphere are activated. When the same monkey hears the crack of a twig, other more general auditory processing circuits in both hemispheres are activated. It is, then, not surprising that for humans also, speech is special, triggering specialized processing mechanisms in the brain. But in processing the communicative acoustic signals of our own species specially, humans are not special. Many other species do an equivalent thing. The argument about whether speech is special should be divided into two different issues: (1) similarities and differences between humans and other species, and (2) similarities and differences, for humans only, between speech processing and the processing of other acoustic stimuli. In the following sections, we will look at relevant data.

Other species' perception of speech

Research has tended to focus either on similarities between human and other mammalian perception of human speech or on differences. In this section, we'll look first at the similarities and then at the differences, with some inferences about the evolution of human speech perception.

One side of the scientific debate emphasizes similarities between human and non-human perception of speech, as discovered in experiments on particular features. One famous experiment showed that chinchillas (a species of rodent) make categorical judgements about certain speech sounds similarly to humans. Categorical perception is judgement of stimuli on a continuous scale as if there were a definite boundary somewhere along the scale, separating two distinct categories. The chinchilla experiment looked at the speech feature known as 'voice onset time' (VOT). VOT is a feature that distinguishes English /p/ from /b/, as in the *pit/bit* alternation, and similarly /t/ from /d/, and /k/ from /g/. Voice is vibration of the vocal cords, as in singing and the pronunciation of vowels and some consonants. Whispered speech is speech without vibration of the vocal cords, i.e. unvoiced or voiceless speech. Consonants in all languages are typically arranged in pairs, with contrastive voiced and voiceless variants. English examples include the /p–b/, /t–d/, /k–g/, /s–z/, and /f–v/ contrasts. The English /p/ phoneme, at the beginning of a word, is pronounced with a short unvoiced puff of air after the lips have parted, known as 'aspiration', and represented phonetically as [p^h]. In pronouncing the English /b/ phoneme at the beginning of a word, the voicing of the following vowel begins simultaneously with, or even just before, the parting of the lips, so there is no audible breathy puff of air. In phonetic parlance, the English /b/ is 'unaspirated'. VOT similarly affects the other plosive contrasts /t–d/ and /k–g/. The difference between aspirated and unaspirated sounds is a matter of degree, because in principle (though not in English fact) the delay (or lack of it) between the parting of the articulators and the onset of voicing can be any number of milliseconds. So stimuli along a continuous scale from clear English /p/ to clear English /b/ can be artificially synthesized and played to subjects. In psychologist Pat Kuhl's experiment, humans and chinchillas were required to make same/different judgements between stimuli very close to each other on this continuous scale. For pairs of stimuli near English /p/, both humans and chinchillas judged them as 'same' (though they were physically slightly different), and likewise for pairs of stimuli close to English /b/, both humans and chinchillas gave 'same' judgements. For pairs of very similar, but not identical, stimuli somewhere in the middle of the scale between /p/ and /b/, humans and chinchillas all made 'different' judgements. Neither the behaviour of the chinchillas nor that of the humans reflected the essential continuous variation in the stimuli. They all made similar categorical judgements. This experiment is a paradigm example of the kind of experiment showing that some aspect of human perception of speech is shared with non-human animals.

Similar experiments by comparative psychologist Ruth Tincoff and colleagues have shown that cotton-top tamarin monkeys make similar judgements to human babies about the rhythm of different languages. Both babies and tamarins distinguished between languages with different rhythmic patterns, such as English and Japanese, or Dutch and Japanese, and noticed no difference between languages of the same rhythmic type, e.g. Dutch and English. How can you tell whether a monkey or a baby distinguishes between two stimuli? They can't make verbal reports. A 'habituation paradigm' is used. One kind of stimulus is played to the subject (monkey or baby) until the subject seems quite used to it, even bored by it. Then another stimulus is played, from a loudspeaker in a different place, and you see if the subject turns its head toward the source of the new stimulus. If it does, this is interpreted as the subject having noticed a difference. If it doesn't, this is interpreted as the subject treating the stimuli as belonging to the same type. These researchers concluded that the speech rhythm detection mechanisms in both tamarin monkeys and human babies are the same, indicating that they are evolutionarily very old, dating at least to the common ancestor of monkeys and humans, at least 30 million years ago.

Another experiment, by primatologists Shozo Kojima and Shigeru Kiritani, established that chimpanzees, like humans, can do 'speaker normalization', at least on a limited set of vowels. The formant values of vowels are somewhat different for men and women, as women have a typically higher fundamental frequency (pitch) than men. Nevertheless, whether a man or a woman says a word, we can recognize it as the same word, even though the formant patterns are different for the different speakers. This is speaker normalization. Kojima and Kiritani found that chimpanzees can do it too, for certain vowels in the low back area, between [ɑ] and [o]. They did not test on other vowels. The capacity to do vocal tract normalization when hearing sounds made by different individual animals within one species has also been attested in Japanese macaques, chinchillas, and dogs.

The data discussed above come from controlled experiments aimed specifically at the issue of speech perception by animals. More anecdotally, it is well known that many non-human species can learn to respond systematically to human speech. Trained apes, dogs, horses, and birds testify to this. Clearly, getting some information out of human speech is possible for them. What we don't know from such cases is how much information the animals are systematically extracting from the signal using the same kind of knowledge, or rules, that humans use, and how much is guesswork based on the context of the signals. Many other layers of language beside phonological structure are involved whenever anyone, human or otherwise, responds appropriately to speech. We don't get any detailed insight into other animals' ways of processing speech at the phonological level from the various experimenters' interactions with the likes of Kanzi, Rico, and Alex.

What about experimentally established differences between human and other species' perception of speech? Chimpanzees have poor auditory working memory. They can't retain a sound in memory for long, whereas, interestingly, they have very good visual working memory. Working-memory retention in both visual and auditory modalities is simply tested by giving the subject two stimuli with a time delay in between, and the subject's task is to indicate whether the stimuli are the same or different. Tested on auditory stimuli, chimps' performance was only at 80% accuracy after a gap of 2 seconds, whereas with visual stimuli, their performance was at 90% accuracy after a gap of as much as 16 seconds. These are among results reported by primatologists Kazuhida Hashiya and Shozo Kojima. Humans diagnosed with Specific Language Impairment are significantly poorer than normal controls at detecting sounds presented close together in time, indicating the important role played by auditory short-term memory in language processing. To take in a passage of fluent speech, short-term storage of sounds is crucial. Sometimes, especially in noisy conditions, you only realize what someone has said a few seconds after you hear it. During the interval, your brain has been reviewing its stored representation of the original sound input. Many experiments by psychologist Joan Sinnott have shown detailed differences between human and non-human hearing of speech; her experimental animals included monkeys and gerbils.

Recognizing speech and other noises

As already mentioned, many primates process the meaningful calls of conspecifics differently from other sounds they hear. There is a left-hemisphere preference for processing the meaningful signals. The salience of the left hemisphere is also potentially significant here, as so much of human language processing also happens in the left hemisphere. A similar difference would not be surprising in humans. Some human brain areas are specialized for voices, as opposed to other kinds of sound. Psychologist Pascal Belin and colleagues used fMRI (functional magnetic resonance imaging) to find areas that respond selectively to voices. They suggest that this is analogous to the existence of specific face recognition areas in the visual system. Further, in the pathological condition 'Pure Word Deafness', perception of speech is impaired, while affected patients manage better to recognize non-speech sounds.

The bifurcation of processing into speech and non-speech implies some sorting of aspects of the input signal. A factor contributing to this sorting is 'auditory scene analysis', a process identifying which sounds come from which objects in the surroundings. In many situations, there are several noise-emitting objects, and it is advantageous to be able to bundle together those aspects of the overall stream coming from a common source. Where one person is speaking against a background of non-human environmental noise such as weather or traffic, this sorting is already a sorting of speech from non-speech. We can all do it. And because human communication is usually more significant to us than other noise, we are better at singling out a human voice than we would be at, say, singling out the song of one bird from that of others in a dawn chorus, although that can also be done by those interested enough in birdsong. Humans can learn to attend selectively to specific features of the input to their ears. As we live in social groups, selectively attending to and analysing spoken input becomes more automatic and routinized than processing of other types of sound. The 'cocktail party effect' also allows some people to selectively attend to the talk of just one speaker in a room crowded with other chatterers.

It appears that our adult dispositions to hearing speech are not just a result of learning to sort out socially significant sounds, especially speech. Newborn babies, no more than four days old, already show a preference for listening to speech over other sounds that are similar to speech in a range of acoustic properties. How can you tell what a newborn baby 'prefers'? An accepted measure in psychology is sucking activity. If a baby sucks more, or more strongly, while experiencing one sound rather than another, this is taken to show a preference. Certainly any difference in sucking activity systematically related to features of the input means that the baby is sensitive to a difference between the stimuli. Psychologists Athena Vouloumanos and Janet Werker gave babies two sorts of stimuli, alternating over 8 minutes, each different stimulus repeated for a minute before switching to the other. One stimulus was the nonsense word *lif* spoken by a woman, the other was a sound carefully crafted to have many of the same acoustic features, including pitch, length, and three formants at a speech-like intensity, but overall still clearly not a sound spoken by a human. The babies, twenty-two of them, did indeed respond differently to the two sorts of sound, sucking more for the real speech stimulus. It's plausible that a disposition to suck more when hearing a human voice (especially a female one) is adaptive and naturally selected. The authors argue against a suggestion that the babies have learned to respond to the pitch patterns of speech in the womb.

Among humans, beside speech, another common type of aural input is music. The brain treats speech and music differently, though there are clearly some shared mechanisms. All cultures have some music, perhaps only sung, often with instruments. Simple music is as basic to human culture as language. But only some individuals can perform well and perceive all the distinctions available in a rich musical tradition. Thus, complex musical ability is not as universal as complex language ability. Music and language both use the acoustic/aural medium, so some common processing is to be expected. But beyond using the basic sensations of frequency, loudness, and rhythm, music and language are structured differently. Research has shown up many detailed differences between the processing of language and music. For example, there are brain-damaged patients who can learn and recite the words of songs, but can't recognize or perform the corresponding melodies. Some aphasic patients can sing songs quite fluently but can't produce fluent grammatical speech. The idea that human language ability evolved out of a prior well-developed musical ability is a non-starter. More likely is that both music and language are special abilities that share some common processing but also have their own dedicated mechanisms. The higher levels of musical and linguistic ability are likely to have evolved quite recently, on separate paths, but building on some common basic capacities.

Music is strongly rhythmical, more so than language, in which rhythm is looser. Interestingly, the range of animals who can bob or tap to the beat of music, either spontaneously or after training, is rather similar to the range of animals who can do vocal learning, i.e. imitate sounds. Alex the parrot could do both, monkeys cannot do either, and nor can apes, apart from us human apes who can do both. It has been suggested that the capacity to induce a rhythmic beat and the capacity for vocal learning, essential for language, build on the same brain mechanisms, though what these are is as yet unclear. This is another case where our closest relatives, other primates, lack some language-related ability that can be found in more distant species, particularly some birds.

It is one thing to be able to recognize speech; it is another to be able to reproduce it. The 'Motor Theory of Speech Perception', proposed by phonetician Alvin Liberman, claims that the acoustic information in speech reaching the ear is automatically translated into articulatory terms. To see how surprising this seems, consider an analogy with written symbols. When we read characters on a page, no responses resembling writing or typing are triggered in our bodies. Speech is more ancient than writing, so it is more possible that some such translation process has been laid down in evolution. Undoubtedly, we are able to imitate speech sounds. Children end up much better imitators of the speech around them than adults, but even with them the imitation is not an instantaneous response; they need plenty of practice.

It has been suggested that the discovery of mirror neurons reinforces the Motor Theory of Speech Perception. Neurons active both when perceiving an action and producing it provide some basis for an explanation of how imitation is possible. The actions involved in the discovery of mirror neurons, such as grasping a peanut, differ from speech in two important ways. Continuous speech, even pronouncing an average-length word, is a series of gestures influencing and blending into each other in complex ways. Furthermore, grasping a peanut is guided by an external target (the peanut), whereas the only 'target' of speech is some auditory memory of what it should sound like.

A strong form of the Motor Theory is that (1) it is intrinsic to speech perception and (2) it applies only to humans. This strong version cannot be sustained. People with severely impaired speech motor capacity often have intact speech perception. An ability to relate heard speech to the motor actions needed to reproduce it is not unique to humans; parrots do it quite well. And animals unable to produce anything like human speech, such as chimpanzees, can perceive some vowels, consonants, and whole words, as we have seen. A weaker form of the theory is that humans are capable, to a far greater degree than non-humans, of both speech perception and production, and that these two capacities mutually reinforce each other in development and in online performance. This mutual reinforcement is adaptive. Thus, a weak version of the Motor Theory is compatible both with the special abilities of humans and with continuity with other species.

Summarizing, humans do have an innate disposition to treat speech sounds differently from other sounds. This initial filter of the auditory input can be used to build other abilities which are learned, including analysis of the spoken input into the phonological objects of a particular language, its phonemes, syllables, tones, edges of words, and intonation contours. Experiments exposing newborn or very young babies to stimuli exemplifying these features, isolated from others, show very early good performance.

6

Coining words

We saw in Chapter 4 how individual non-human animals can have mental representations, which I cautiously called 'proto-concepts', which are sometimes rather abstract, going well beyond mere reflex stimulus–response connections. These can be learned, and are not necessarily innate. Non-human animals, at a certain evolved level, have rich mental lives, a kind of natural intelligence that allows them to negotiate their world well. But, with the exception of the largely innate alarm and food calls of monkeys and apes, these mental representations are not put to any communicative use between animals. Such mental organization is almost entirely for private, selfish use. In Chapter 3 we surveyed what preconditions it takes for a communicative code to get set up in a social group. These prerequisites included norms of cooperativeness within the group, shared intentions, reciprocal altruism, and trust. In this chapter I will assume that all this was established in our prehistory. Humans are now ready to go public with their thoughts, sharing them to the benefit of others, the group, and indirectly themselves.

An ability to learn some vocabulary necessarily precedes any ability to make sentence-like strings out of it according to conventional rules. Trained apes can learn vocabulary, up to a couple of hundred signs in American Sign Language (ASL), but they show hardly any ability to master the ASL rules of combination. A trained chimpanzee, Sarah, had to learn a small vocabulary of coloured plastic tokens, standing for objects and actions, before she could understand some strings of these arranged in a conventional order. Language-ready modern children learn vocabulary voraciously before they begin to make grammatical utterances several words long. So we presume that in the origins of language a one-word stage preceded our remote ancestors' first steps into grammar. The term 'protolanguage' has been widely used to describe this one-word stage, where there is vocabulary but no grammar.

In the context of evolution, 'What?' and 'How?' questions naturally arise. 'What?' questions can be asked about both the meanings and the forms of the early vocabulary. A 'What?' question about the form of early words is whether they were manual gestures or vocalizations—a question I'll discuss later in this chapter. We can also ask how the earliest spoken words are likely to have been pronounced. Probably the first spoken forms were simple syllables of a [pa, ti, go] sort, and we'll get to that question in more detail in Chapter 8, our last chapter. A 'What?' question about meaning is whether the meanings of the first conventionally signifying forms were typically types of object (e.g. rock, lion) or actions (e.g. run, fight), or even, as some have suggested, whole event types (e.g. giving food to someone) or types of state of affairs (e.g. there is a lion behind a rock). We'll consider that in the next section.

What did the first words mean?

How did the very first vocabularies arise? We are concerned here with learned pairings between meanings and forms, not with instinctive unlearned pairings as in the alarm calls of monkeys and birds and the food calls of some apes. For convenience, I'll call these meaning–form pairings 'words', but keep in mind that the unitary elements that were first used were not words in the modern sense of fitting into a conventional grammar. It makes no sense, for example, to ask whether the first words were nouns or verbs, because nouns and verbs are only fully defined within a framework of grammar. A different, question is whether the first words typically signified objects, actions, or whole events, a matter of meaning.

Many animals use calls to 'do things to each other', in the words of Chapter 3. There are mating calls, threat calls, territorial calls, calls to keep contact with the group, 'signature' calls identifying individuals, and so on. In an early human group, with more developed social arrangements than their precursor apes, we can assume some continuation of signals serving essentially these dyadic purposes, i.e. just used for interaction between people, but without referring to any outside thing or situation. So some of the first words were surely of this type, surviving in English words such as *Hi*, *Sorry*, *Thanks*, *Ugh*, and *Phew*. In modern languages, such words are relatively few, compared to our huge vocabularies of words with descriptive content. In their modern adapted way, such dyadic doing-things-to-each-other words reflect pre-human communication and have evolved and survived into modern languages. But how did the rest of the vocabularies of languages arise, with eventually tens of thousands of items signifying things and events in the world talked about by the communicators?

I explained earlier a distinction between 'cued' brain activity immediately tied to the current situation and 'detached' brain activity not directly stimulated by the immediate situation. An interesting parallel exists with the different ways in which words can carry meaning. The meanings of some words are rooted in the situation in which they are used. These are known as 'deictic' or 'indexical' words. For example, the English pronouns *this* and *that* are used to refer to, or point to, things in the immediate context of a conversation, and so to different things on different occasions. I might use *that* referring to a dog, or a house, or a mountain, or a wave, and so on. What *that* means depends on where and when it is used. By contrast, words such as *dog*, *house*, *mountain*, and *wave* mean, respectively, the concepts DOG, HOUSE, MOUNTAIN, and WAVE, regardless of where and when they are used. Both types of meaning are useful. It is useful to be able to refer concisely to things present here and now. Sometimes one doesn't know a word for something crucially important to a message. The deictic word *you* is useful just because it is not permanently attached to any one person. On the other hand, continuing informative discourse over many years in a community needs a firm structure of words whose meanings are relatively constant. The essence of communication is to publicly relate current situations to past experience. This is so intrinsic in the nature of communication that we can assume that the earliest forms of language had both kinds of word, deictic and 'universal'.

Was the first protolanguage holistic or atomistic? That is, did single words signify whole quite complex situations, involving several participants and a relation between them, as in MAN-GIVE-MEAT-TO-WOMAN (the holistic option)? Or did the first words signify single concepts of individual objects or actions, such as common things and stuff (e.g. MAN, MEAT) and types of action or relation (e.g. GIVE)? This latter is the atomistic option. The atomistic option, and specifically a version favouring object types, is on the whole more likely. The main evidence comes from preferences shown by modern children in their vocabulary learning. Children learn the meanings of many of their first words during episodes in which both child and caregiver pay joint attention to the same object. Now any object attended to is likely to be involved in some action or in some relationship with other parts of the scene. When a child is shown a teddy-bear, the bear is likely to be in someone's hand, or being moved in some way. Why doesn't the child assume that *teddy* means something like MUMMY-SHAKING-A-TOY-BEAR? Psychologists studying word-learning in children have concluded that they make a 'Whole Object Assumption'. In a scenario of rather deliberate word-teaching by a parent, this is very plausible. Mummy would show a bear and say *teddy*, show an apple and say *apple*, Daddy would say *teddy* while picking the bear up, and *apple* while about to munch an apple, and so on. What can be distilled out of such situations is a correlation between a single whole object type (it need not always be the same apple) and a word. In less overtly didactic situations, children observing the usage around them are likely to distil out names for specific object types. The phenomenon has been labelled 'Cross Situational Learning'. A further conclusion about children learning vocabulary is that they follow a 'Taxonomic Assumption', whereby the meanings of words are expected by the child to classify the entities they see in the world, thereby arriving at the meanings we assume for such words as *dog*, *baby*, *spoon*, and so on.

From a range of different observed situations involving some of the same meanings and some of the same words, children first learn correlations between words and whole object types. The majority of words in the first 100 learned by children refer to types of object. It seems likely that the first protolanguage was atomistic in the relation between meanings and forms. (Don't take the term 'atomistic' too literally—it's not a claim that the atoms of perception of the world are whole objects.)

Linguist Merritt Ruhlen has been far bolder than others in asserting that one can discern modern echoes of the very earliest meaning–form pairs. He has proposed, on the basis of far-reaching comparisons, twenty-six 'global etymologies', claimed to represent the earliest words used by humans. Two of these proposed early forms are *TIK, with a range of meanings including ONE and FINGER, and *PAL, claimed to have meant TWO. Something like these would have been words used by populations of early humans even before their move out of Africa. Ruhlen's methods are less strict than those conventionally adopted by historical linguists, who are almost unanimously sceptical of his claims.

In summary, a few of the earliest words would have had pure 'illocutionary' doing-things-to-each-other meanings, like *Hello*, and very many others would have had descriptive content, with a bias toward naming types of individual objects, e.g. *child*, *cave*, *stick*. And we should add that at some stage (there's no knowing when) words began to have affective connotations—compare *urinate* with *piss* or *guerrilla* with *terrorist*.

Visible gestures or audible speech?

Words can come out in different ways. They can be spoken, signed, or written. We will hardly be concerned with written language, as writing only emerged in human history about 5,000 years ago, long after spoken languages of some kind had been around for probably over 100 millennia. Here, we will explore the question of whether words first evolved in a spoken or manually signed form.

Although the vast majority of modern languages are spoken, a significant number of manually signed languages exist as the primary language of some people, almost exclusively deaf people. Signed languages of the deaf, when they are historically developed and not still in an embryonic stage, are just as expressive and complex as spoken languages. I became dramatically aware of this at a conference on quite abstruse theoretical aspects of syntax and semantics, where I found the spoken talks pretty hard going, because of their abstractness and complexity. The talks were simultaneously translated into American Sign Language (ASL) by an interpreter, for the benefit of deaf people in the audience. Some deaf people asked technical questions, in ASL, their questions were translated into English, and a spoken reply was given and translated back into ASL. I found these technical exchanges just as challenging to follow, because of the difficulty of their content, as many of the spoken talks at the conference. Clearly ASL equips its users with a range of abstractions and nuances comparable to those of spoken languages. The more general message is that underlying the medium in which language is expressed, whether signed or spoken, is a system which is independent of the medium. Language, though expressed in concrete physical utterances, has layers of structure that are not tied to any one physical medium. For the distant origins of language, we can then ask whether speech was always the dominant medium in which it was expressed, or whether manual signs were once equally, or perhaps even more, used as the output modality.

In the modern era, the 'Gesture Theory of Language Origin' was first advocated by anthropologist Gordon Hewes in the 1970s. Support for the theory has increased in recent decades, perhaps in part due to a growing awareness of the status of sign languages as full languages. Previously, many had believed that sign languages were no more than the ad hoc gestures that a tourist may invent to get by in a foreign country. This is wrong. Rudimentary systems of 'home sign' are often invented in households with a deaf child of hearing parents who have no access to a proper sign language. Home sign systems have limited expressive scope and are not standardized in a larger community. Deaf sign languages, on the other hand, have comparable expressive power to spoken languages. This makes it more appealing to wonder whether the first languages used by humans were manually signed, rather than spoken.

Even in mature sign languages, there are more examples of an iconic relationship between form and meaning than in spoken languages, in which, apart from a few onomatopoeic words, the relationship is essentially arbitrary. The meanings of verbs for different types of movement in spoken languages are usually not transparent. We can't tell, just by the sound of the words, what kind of motion is indicated by *walk, run, swim, fly,* or *crawl.* But in sign languages, some iconicity has often been retained, and the meanings of the signs for these motion-types can be more successfully guessed at. The hands can also be used to mime the shape of many physical objects, and signs for objects are still often iconic in this sense in sign languages. Instinctive facial expressions, as for pleasure or disgust, can also be readily adapted to convey such meanings in a conventional way. In a group of people just beginning to signal meanings to each other, many more meanings could be guessed from manual and facial gestures than from attempts to express them vocally. It would be easier to get a gestural language off the ground in the first place than a speech-based one.

Humans are predominantly right-handed, and the left hemisphere of the brain controls skilled right-hand movements. In the great majority of people, the left hemisphere also houses the major sites of language processing, in brain regions such as Broca's area and Wernicke's area. Chimpanzees show some evidence of a bias to right-handedness, including in their meaningful gestures. And chimpanzees use voluntarily controlled manual and facial gestures more for communication than their vocalizations, which are more automatic, reflecting fear or anger. There is also some evidence that meaningful gestures vary from one chimpanzee group to another and are culturally transmitted (in the limited sense in which chimpanzee groups have cultures). In chimpanzee and macaque brains, there are anatomical analogues of the human Broca's area, a crucial language-related area in humans. In macaques, this area includes the mirror neurons that correlate observation of gestures with their production. In chimpanzees, this brain area does not control vocalizations. In humans, there is still some overlap between the brain's responses to meaningful speech and meaningful gestures. Putting all this together, a plausible story can be told of the recruitment of the communicative gesture areas of our primate ancestors' brains for communicative speech.

The gesture story need not be an all-or-nothing account. Possibly both modes of communication coexisted, and perhaps interacted with each other. A transition from mainly gestural language to predominantly spoken language could have been gradual. We still gesticulate while speaking (though our gesticulations are not the conventional signs of sign languages). The spoken medium has several advantages, once a spoken code is up and running. Speech can be used in the dark, addressed to people behind you, around corners, and while the hands are otherwise occupied. Another advantage of articulate speech is that it is not obviously practically useful for anything other than communication. Waving your hands about might be supposed to be intended to ward off insects, certain signs could be confused with scratching an itch, fanning one's brow, or rubbing the hands for warmth. Making articulate speech sounds, by contrast, seems practically pointless, unless the sounds have some symbolic significance. This is an argument based on the idea of signalling signalhood, discussed in previous chapters.

It is known that full sign languages can spring up in deaf communities in a matter of a few generations, as we have seen with Nicaraguan Sign Language and Al-Sayyid Bedouin Sign Language. Our ancestors were not deaf, but at one time they lacked spoken language, so it is not beyond imagination that the first glimmerings of human language were in the manual gestural medium. Nevertheless, in the final chapters we will focus on the origins of speech, as the current dominant medium in which language is expressed.

Articulate sounds emerge

The International Phonetic Association (IPA) publishes a single A4 sheet of paper setting out the speech sounds for which it has devised symbols, the International Phonetic Alphabet. There are just over a hundred of them; phoneticians call them phonetic 'segments'. And the IPA also defines a small number of 'diacritics' representing slight modifications of the basic sound segments. This A4 sheet is the bible for beginning phonetics students. These are all the sounds you may encounter in the world's languages, they are told. Learn to recognize them and to make them, and you'll be an accomplished articulatory phonetician. Basic phonetics classes can be fun or daunting. More adventurous students enjoy straining their tongues and lips and controlling their breathing in novel ways to produce unaccustomed speech sounds. Phonetics classes are also an exercise in fine hearing discrimination. These classes usually take the IPA chart of sounds as the curriculum. The impression can be gained that exactly this set of sounds exists timelessly as a complete inventory of natural phonetic types, like the periodic table of chemical elements.

We are used to thinking about speech sounds in terms of the alphabet. Apart from the oddities of English spelling, one letter corresponds to one sound, we assume. Written letters were invented by humans, using convenient resources, such as pen, ink, and paper, or stylus and clay, and designed to be easy to write and tell apart. In a practical system, written symbols should be made with straightforward gestures, or simple combinations of gestures resulting in clearly defined images on the medium. Written symbols also shouldn't be too numerous, placing too large a burden on learning and memory. Finally, in a cursive (joined-up) script the letters should still be individually discernible in the continuous flow across the page. Now, speech sounds should be thought of in a similar way to the letters in a cursive script. Though not consciously invented, they have evolved under similar pressures of usability, i.e. to be relatively easy to produce as a speaker, and to distinguish as a hearer, all in a continuous joined-up stream of sound. The resources involved are the possibilities afforded by the anatomy of the human vocal tract and physiology of its control. Humans may, when drunk, dreaming, or delirious, make noises with their vocal tract that are 'inarticulate'. In inarticulate vocalizing, the various parts of the vocal tract are not coordinated so as to produce the crisply discernible sounds found in careful deliberate speech. The elements of articulate speech, in all languages, have evolved to be just that, articulate, i.e. easy to tell apart in the stream of speech, and in such numbers as not to be too hard to learn and control.

There are many degrees of freedom in the vocal tract. The lips can be more or less protruded, the jaw can be at various heights, parts of the tongue (tip, blade, body, back) can be moved somewhat independently, giving different tongue shapes, the velum (soft palate) can be raised or lowered to allow or block airflow through the nose, the vocal cords may vibrate at different pitches or be held wide open, or close off completely, the larynx housing the vocal cords may be raised or lowered, sometimes acting as a piston to force air upward, and so on. This is just a beginning sketch of the possibilities. Speech is like the coordination of a small orchestra, performing to a 'gestural score', with a separate line of the score for each movable part of the vocal tract. Following the orchestral metaphor, each separate articulator is an instrument, and they must all work together in controlled ways to produce articulate speech. If each articulator were randomly activated to move independently of the others, the result would resemble an orchestra tuning up cacophonously, not coherent articulate speech. Something like this happens in babies 'cooing' behaviour, and the earliest stages of babbling, after which they start to produce recognizable phonetic segments. Articulate speech needs a conductor, a motor programme organizing coordination of the movements of the vocal tract. Through cooing and babbling, babies learn to orchestrate the movements of their vocal tracts and articulate the sounds of their native language.

The sound systems of modern languages are mature, using phonetic segments that have been learned and passed on by successive generations. The languages of the world long ago settled into using fairly stable subsets of the sounds listed on the IPA chart. The phonetic changes seen in modern languages show rather little evolution of the set of possible sounds that languages use. (See 'The next consonants and a new vowel' in Chapter 8.) But considering speech in the light of evolution, and knowing that our closest primate relatives have no appreciable vocal articulatory skill, we can ask two basic intertwined questions, a biological one and a cultural one. The biological question of how our species evolved such vocal versatility, making us 'speech-ready', was discussed earlier in the sections on the evolution of the vocal tract and its control. The cultural question is how, in communities of speech-ready people at the dawn of language, conventional inventories of speech sounds evolved to be the phoneme sets of their languages. Inarticulate random movements of the vocal tract are not useful for communication. Populations of communicators need to find stable points in the phonetic landscape, conveniently produced and reliably recognized combinations of the articulators, as building blocks for their vocabulary. It is a process of phonetic order emerging out of a situation which could equally have produced only phonetic chaos.

The question of what kinds of mechanism led to the emergence of phonetic segments from the 'phonetic soup' that random innervation of the vocal tract would give has been explored in a rather abstract way by computer modellers. Cognitive scientists Bart de Boer and Jelle Zuidema constructed a model simulating the pressures that most plausibly lead to the emergence of phonetic segments out of the space of possibilities offered by independent movements of articulators. The goal of the simulation was to find a small set of points within this space that are maximally distinct from each other. The natural assumption is that the speech sounds actually used by humans are distinct enough from each other to facilitate communication. Sounds too similar to each other would not be useful. The simulation started with a small fixed number of random movements through the idealized phonetic space, like random walks, simulating a chaotic state of inarticulacy, like that of a delirious person or a pre-babbling baby. Now a 'hill-climbing' algorithm was applied, tending to change the movements so as to make them as distinct from each other as possible. The pressure to find a set of combinations of movements clearly distinct from each other produces, it is claimed, the sets of distinct speech sounds that languages end up using. It seems a reasonable account of the rise of phonetic segments, those 'sounds' that are singled out by the IPA chart as being the ones that languages use. This is a story of the evolutionary emergence of phonetic articulateness.

Like most computer models, this model severely simplified the actual state of affairs in the vocal tract, but nevertheless demonstrates a process that can be fairly assumed to apply in more complex circumstances.

The degrees of freedom in the vocal tract make for a high-dimensional space of possibilities. A process of selecting a set of maximally distant points in such a multidimensional landscape is not deterministic. That means that, depending on slight differences in the initial conditions, and given some small amount of random-ness in the process, different sets of segments will be settled on in different cases. The different sets of segments arrived at will overlap substantially, containing many of the most common sounds found in the world's languages. The process of phonetic segments emerging can be thought of as the way in which the earliest languages would have formed their sets of phonemes, their distinctive units of sound. In the course of the histories of languages phonemes come to be modified in certain ways, and we will later see ways in which the phonemic systems of more mature languages differ from those that were probably typical of the earliest languages.

That, above, was a model of how an inventory of distinct phonetic segments emerges from the potential confusion of available noises that can be made by the vocal tract. In that model, those sounds were selected so as to be as distinct from each other as possible. There are two 'axes' in the systematic structure of languages, which are usefully called the axes of 'choice' and 'chain'. The model described in the last section was about selection of sounds distinct from each other on the axis of choice. The sounds that emerged make a list from which languages can 'choose' to form their words. As a real example, slightly simplified, the inventory of phonemes in Hawaiian is the unusually small set { m, n, p, t, ?, h, w, l, i, e, a, o, u }. (? is the phonetic symbol for a glottal stop.) Here, you will notice, there are eight consonant phonemes and five vowel phonemes. Words in Hawaiian are made from just this small set. But we haven't said anything yet that excludes such crazily fictitious Hawaiian words as /ptnlw/, a sequence of five consonants and no vowels, or /aiueo/, a sequence of five vowels and no consonants. Some languages do indeed cluster large numbers of consonants together with no intervening vowels, but this is rare, and severely limited in those languages. English is quite permissive in this respect, with words like *splints*, phonetically [splɪnts], starting and ending with clusters of three consonants. This is unusual among languages. In general, words in languages are formed so that sounds are as distinct from each other as possible along the chain axis. That is, not only should every sound be well distinct from others that might go in the same place in a word (e.g. as the first sound), but also well distinct from its neighbours in the chain forming the word. Consonants are easier to distinguish when they are surrounded by vowels.

This gives rise to the most basic syllable structure found in languages: a single consonant followed by a single vowel, abbreviated by linguists to 'CV'. Every language has syllables of this basic CV sort, and some languages have only this kind of syllable. Hawaiian is a language coming close to this extreme of simple syllable structure. You never get two consonants together in Hawaiian, though you can get two vowels together, making a diphthong or a lengthened vowel. Here are some Hawaiian words: *maka* 'eye', *wahine* 'woman', *kanaka* 'man', *kalikimaka* 'Christmas'. Observe that these all have CV structure only. The last example shows what Hawaiian must do when borrowing a word from a language with more complex syllable structure (and more consonants to choose from). Yoruba, a language of West Africa, also comes close to having only CV syllables, with the result that words borrowed from other languages often get simplified. Examples of English loans to Yoruba are *pirifeti* 'prefect', and *sikolasipu* 'scholarship'. Note the consistent CV patterns here.

Phonetician Peter McNeilage has suggested that the ultimate ancient origin of basic CV syllable structure is the rhythmic opening-and-closing jaw movements carried out by all mammals and birds in such ordinary non-communicative activities as chewing and suckling. Many animal cries start with an opening of the mouth, followed by a vocalization made with the mouth open. A mouth-opening gesture accompanied by vocalization is one of the simplest things the vocal tract can do. If one reduces a stream of speech to its most basic components, eliminating all the differences between consonants and all the differences between vowels, one is left with a sequence, quite rhythmic, of successive openings and closings of the mouth—primitive syllables. Indeed, speaking is jokingly called 'chin-wagging'. Modern speech has superimposed exquisite levels of differentiated control on top of this basic rhythmic action.

So it is reasonable to speculate that the syllable structure of the earliest languages was CV only, and that more complex syllable structures, as in English, Russian, and the Tashlhiyt Berber language of North Africa, emerged later as historical developments. (Tashlhiyt is plausibly argued to have some syllables entirely without vowels, e.g. *tqssf* 'it shrunk (fem)' and *tfktstt* 'you gave it (fem)'. On the face of it, such words would be very difficult to perceive accurately, especially with the doubled consonants in them.)

In a famous work, linguist Roman Jakobson drew attention to a hierarchy of types of syllable structure, with the CV type at its bottom end. Jakobson connected three areas of study that one might think are only distantly related, namely child language, aphasia, and phonological universals. Not only is CV the most basic syllable type, found in all languages, but it is also the first kind of syllable produced by children learning a language, and is the type of syllable that severely aphasic patients regress to. Both children and aphasic patients simplify syllable structure. My daughter Rosie simplified *chocolate* to [koko]. Another child simplified *Patrick* to [baba]. (Repetition of the same syllable is also typical of early child speech.) Some parents disparage words like *doggie* as 'baby language', but *doggie*, with its repeated CV pattern, has the advantage for the child of coming more naturally than *dog*, with its final consonant. Parents needn't worry; it's a stage that children naturally pass through, on their way to acquiring more complex syllables, if their language has them. Paul Broca, a nineteenth-century pioneer of aphasia research, had an unfortunate patient whose only utterance was a repeated CV syllable, spelt *tan-tan* in French. Recent research has found this to be a common pattern among severe aphasic patients; one patient could only produce [mama], another [dodo]. (Note again the repetition of a syllable.) Jakobson's idea was that there is a scale of naturalness, of the ease with which syllable types can be produced, and that this scale is seen in all three domains, child language, aphasia, and phonological universals. Jakobson's hierarchy is:

First: CV as in *Ma* and *Pa*,
next: V as in *Oh*, or CVC as in *Dad*,
last: VC as in *am*, or CCV as in *bra*, or CVCC as in *past*.

In both child language and aphasia, there is a 'first in, last out' pattern. The first syllable patterns used by children are the last to be lost by aphasic patients. It seems reasonable to add a fourth domain to Jakobson's three: the evolution of phonological systems from simple beginnings. Thus this hierarchy can be taken to show the order in which more complex syllables probably arose in the earliest languages, if they progressed past the basic CV stage. This is just the skeleton of a large body of knowledge on scales of naturalness in speech, also dealing with the particular combinations that are preferred over others.

Groups converge on arbitrary signs

Now we'll address a 'How?' question about the earliest vocabulary, a question which actually logically precedes the atomistic/holistic issue. This is the question of how a group without any shared learned vocabulary could begin to develop one. How does a vocabulary of any kind emerge from a situation with no vocabulary at all?

In any language, for the vast majority of words, you can't tell what a word means by what it sounds like. As linguists put it, the pairings between meanings and forms are 'arbitrary'. The main exceptions are onomatopoeic words such as *cuckoo* and Spanish *coquí*, the name for a kind of frog that makes a two-note call, first high-pitched then low-pitched. Apart from the calls of animals, there is little scope for meanings that can be naturally conveyed in this way by vocal mimicry. (But manual gestures have some advantage, as we will see in the next section.) How did the first arbitrary pairings of meanings and speech sounds get established as the conventional code of a group?

We have seen a crucial first step in Chapter 3, in the emergence of the phenomenon of 'signalling signalhood'. By this step, an action becomes divorced from its natural meaning (in Grice's terms). If a hunter wanted to attract a female cuckoo (for some bizarre reason) he might make as realistic an imitation of the cuckoo's call as possible. But if a person wants to convey something about a cuckoo to another person, the intention to communicate something comes out in some artificiality of the sound made—it should sound like a person imitating a cuckoo, rather than completely like a cuckoo. The conventional signal is now free to evolve somewhat away from sounding just like a cuckoo. The words for CUCKOO in different languages are different, and conform to the phonological patterns of the languages, which take it away from the original bird's call.

At this stage in our account, we have not yet seen a way in which completely arbitrary signs can emerge, and (to be frank) we don't have much detailed idea about how it could have happened. One possibility is that some naturally occurring 'synaesthetic' connections between objects and some of their properties were exploited. Some people even today are natural synaesthetes. They make clearly felt associations between things which other people don't make. Some synaesthetes, for example, associate numbers with colours (e.g. 3 is red), letters with tastes ('O' is salty), sounds with smells (a violin note smells like roses), and so on. Some extreme synaesthetes cannot easily suppress these associations, which can become problematic in their lives. Most people feel some synaesthetic associations. I have asked classes of students what colour is suggested by the high front [i] vowel in the word *bee*, and a significant number say it brings yellow to mind. To me, the [u] vowel in *do* is brownish. Musicians talk of 'bright' sounds, and 'sharp' and 'flat' notes, applying visual and tactile properties to sounds.

A well-known, but rather too informal, experiment shows people two shapes on card; one is a jagged shape with sharp points, the other is rounded, cloudlike with no points. Subjects are then asked which shape they would naturally label *kiki* and which they would label *bouba*. You won't be surprised to learn that overwhelmingly the jagged shape is labelled *kiki* and the rounded shape *bouba*.

Psychologist Christine Cuskley has shown that this result is probably unfairly influenced by the shape of the letters, *k*, which is spiky, and *b*, which is rounded. But many other experiments do shown genuine connections between things and features perceived by different senses. (The cases most relevant to language origins involve speech sounds, not written letters, of course.)

Some synaesthesia-like correlations occur repeatedly in languages, suggesting a naturalness to connections that otherwise might be deemed arbitrary. These correlations are not absolute, but hold with high statistical significance. I will illustrate three of them. Across languages, there is a statistical tendency for words describing small size, weakness, lightness, or thinness to use a high front vowel such as [i] as in *bee*. Think of the rhetorical effect of *teeny weeny*, while remembering that this is only a statistical generalization, with counterexamples. Contrastingly, low or back vowels, [a, u], as in *man* and *moon* tend to be associated with large size, heaviness, and strength. Proper names for female people are statistically more likely to have high front [i]-like vowels than names for males. Languages all have 'deictic' pronoun systems, as ways of indicating near things and far-off things; English *this* and *that* make the general point nicely. Across languages, there is a strong statistical tendency for pronouns for near things to have high front [i]-like vowels, and pronouns for far-away things to have vowels made with a lower tongue position, such as [a]. Deictic pronouns are central to communication in everyday situations, and conceivably our early *Homo* ancestors happened on some common simple words relying on a shared synaesthetic association. Then the conventionally established words could have undergone phonetic changes, as words in languages do, making their connection with their meanings more arbitrary. This takes us a little way into how some arbitrary connections between meanings and sounds could have arisen, but admittedly not very far, as it leaves the vast bulk of the vocabulary undiscussed.

Once some vocal noise (or manual gesture) has become recognized across a community as conventionally carrying some specific meaning, the forces of economy and convenience begin to act on the form. We will see in the final chapter how the sounds of languages adapt themselves to be comfortably spoken and easily recognized. Forms get eroded and stylized for ease of use, and this takes them further from any original natural (e.g. onomatopoeic) connection with their meaning. We can see this in the history of ideographic writing systems, like Chinese. For example, the sign for HILL or MOUNTAIN once looked like three triangles, clearly iconic of mountain peaks. Now that sign has been simplified to three upright strokes on a horizontal base line, looking much less like mountains, but being easier to draw with quick brush or pen strokes. Cognitive scientists Nic Fay and Bruno Galantucci have reproduced this kind of simplifying and stylizing effect in the lab, in separate experiments. Fay's and Galantucci's experiments deal with forms drawn on paper rather than spoken forms, but the principles of how stylized forms quickly get established in a group of users are the same as for speech.

Fay got people to try to communicate concepts like THEATRE, CARTOON, and POVERTY by drawings. They were not allowed to talk or gesticulate. At first, their drawings were complex, with many iconic elements. But after a very short period of the subjects exchanging messages, these complex drawings got simplified, often down to a few strokes, and in no way like the original complex forms. People take very easily to memorizing connections between such simple forms and their meanings, if the meanings are reinforced by constant use.

Galantucci had his subjects, in separate rooms, communicate via a computer link, using only a very limited medium of a pen on a moving belt of paper. The movement of the paper made it impossible for the subjects to actually draw pictures or form known alphabetic letters. Their task was to agree to 'meet' in a particular sector of a diagram on their screens. At the beginning, they had no established system of communication. They made it up as they went along, but only communicating via this very limited medium of the moving scroll. And almost all pairs of subjects managed to forge a set of communicative conventions in this very stark set-up. Where there's a will there's a way. These experimental subjects were modern, cooperatively minded humans, with an incentive to succeed in the communicative task, in the absence of any initial given communicative code. Our earliest human ancestors needed to have the will to communicate cooperatively. Given this, and the necessary memory and mental processing capacities, getting a shared code up and running is apparently not difficult. The communal code that emerges is tailored to usefulness, in the sense of making plenty of meaningful distinctions, and with each symbol (because that is what they now are) being easy to produce and distinguish from others. In the last chapter, we will see in more detail how this has made the pronunciation systems of languages what they are today.

The suggested progression thus far in the evolution of the first shared vocabularies starts with non-arbitrary (e.g. onomatopoeic or synaesthetic) connections between words and their meanings. Then through frequent use, words get eroded and fitted, Procrustes-like, into the sound systems of their languages, so that the connections with meaning are more arbitrary. (Procrustes, in Greek mythology, fitted his guests to his bed by lengthening or shortening the guests, rather than adapting the bed.) New learners may not even be aware of any natural connection between the new conventional forms and their meanings, and just learn them without any help from onomatopoeia or synaesthesia. Modern children are ace performers at this. Once it becomes possible to learn large numbers of arbitrary meaning–form connections, the way is open for the vocabulary to expand enormously. Although at the very start of languages, non-arbitrary connections with meaning may have been adaptive in the way I have outlined, as soon as our ancestors became able to memorize arbitrary connections, the very arbitrariness itself was adaptive. This is because it is not possible to imagine a workable vocabulary of thousands of words, all based on some natural connection with their meaning. Most meanings that we want to express just don't have any natural phonetic form that might evoke them.

Modern humans can store tens of thousands of words, whole pairings of meanings with forms. The raw memorizing power involved in mastering a modern language is uniquely human. Some experimental animals have surprised us in how many words they can learn. Kanzi, the trained bonobo, knows all the 256 symbols on his lexigram board, plus some more. Rico, a border collie dog, is reliably attested to have learned over 200 words for things that he can go and fetch on a command from his owner. That's Rico's only use of these words; he doesn't speak them, of course, and he only understands them embedded in a routinized *Fetch* command. The champion performer so far is another border collie dog, Chaser, who, after three years of intensive training has learned over 1,000 words. Humans are obviously much better, both quantitatively, in the numbers of vocabulary items they can learn, and in the versatile use they put them to, both in speaking and hearing and in combining them productively into complex sentences. And we don't need focused training; we just absorb new words like a sponge. These modern human abilities have evolved from numerically lower levels that non-human animals are capable of. It is tempting to see this as at least part of the cause of modern humans' exceptionally large brains. There would have been co-evolution of socially developing shared vocabularies in groups and brain size. This, assumes, plausibly I think, that there was some advantage to individuals in commanding a large vocabulary. Brain tissue is expensive to maintain, so our large brains are unlikely to have expanded by an unmotivated accident.

The possibilities for continued natural connections between meanings and forms are greater in manually signed languages. This is shown by the inspiring story of Nicaraguan Sign Language (NSL), a new language which emerged over some twenty years during the 1970s and 1980s, and which fortunately researchers were on hand to watch growing, year by year. Deaf Nicaraguan children were gathered together for the first time in a school where they interacted with other deaf kids of their own approximate age. In their homes, they had sometimes used 'homesign', simple systems for communicating with hearing family members. Homesign is limited in its expressive power, has little or no conventional grammar, and is not shared by a wider community. Once in the deaf school, the Nicaraguan children very quickly started spontaneously to develop a more powerful language (with no encouragement from the school's teachers), with larger vocabulary, and growing grammatical conventions. The social conditions facilitating this development included: a large enough group of children aged from very young to puberty, and a constant turnover of new young arrivals. The dynamic involved invention by current members of the group followed by quick learning of invented signs by incoming new children. Within twenty years researchers judged that a fully fledged sign language had evolved, comparable in complexity with older sign languages such as ASL and British Sign Language (BSL). As researchers were on hand through this evolutionary process, it was possible to trace the stages of evolution. Children of the early cohorts, when the language was only just getting started, attained some fluency in a rather simple proto-form of the emerging language, and later in life did not master the complexities that subsequently evolved. Children who came to the school later were exposed to a more developed language, and if they were young enough, acquired it well. This tight cycle continued, and the language itself grew.

NSL is a spectacular example, the best existing case, of a new language getting started literally from nothing. Other cases exist, in mixed communities of hearing and deaf people, as in Al-Sayyid Bedouin Sign Language, but the emergence of a new language is slower in these cases and the emerging language is less well rooted as the main language of a social group. As the Nicaraguan children were all deaf, they could get no clue from any of the spoken language around them. They were in a protective environment with good motivation to interact with their peers, and young enough to make it happen. For the considerations of this chapter, the NSL case shows how easy it is for modern, biologically language-ready young humans, given the right social conditions, to get a working shared conventional vocabulary up and running in a very short time. The greater iconic potential of the manual/visual medium, as opposed to the spoken/aural one, no doubt helped substantially. The NSL researchers report how early signs were often iconic, but later became stylized and more arbitrary. This is common in the history of other sign languages. The fast growth of a shared vocabulary in NSL was a striking start. But what was even more amazing was the rapid progress to an organized grammar, to which we will come in Chapter 7.

Words affect thought

We have seen in Chapter 4 how non-human animals have private concepts of things and events in the world around them. They think their way around their environments in wordless ways. Analogous human instances of practical wordless thought could include when we quickly consider whether to cross the road before an oncoming car gets near, or change our mind about which path to take to the shops. (At least I often do those things without ever being aware of relevant words entering my head.) And so far in this chapter we have considered how in a social group public labels, words, get attached to these concepts, so that a whole community now has a shared set of associations between words and concepts. Some thoughts require words, as when we rehearse a list of six things to bring from another room; naming the things, and saying *six* to ourselves. It can happen *sotto voce*, of course. In this section we will see how getting words for things can actually change our thoughts about them.

Individuals vary in their experiences. So the private concepts formed by each person, if based only on their own experience, will not be identical with the private concepts of others. From the food you grow up with as a child, you form a certain concept of FOOD. Children in other families with different cultural backgrounds will have a different concept of FOOD, formed from what they habitually eat. When you get together with other people and talk about food, the private concepts have to be adjusted, in this case probably extended by everyone to include stuff that they had not previously thought of as food. Some experiments with young children show how the very application of a public label will apparently affect how they mentally sort the things they are dealing with.

Babies can be tested for the significant categories that they distinguish by seeing whether they attend more when a stimulus is changed. For instance, show a baby a picture of a rabbit, then replace it with a picture of a pig, and see if the baby looks longer than normal at the new picture. Prolonged looking time is taken to indicate that the baby has noticed a difference. If the baby does not notice a difference, it is concluded that the stimuli belong to the same mental category for the baby. Now add to this experiment spoken labels accompanying each picture, different labels (e.g. *rabbit* and *pig*) for each stimulus. In this case, babies notice differences more than they did in the unlabelled condition. This was research done by psychologists Marie Balaban and Sandra Waxman on 9-month-old babies. This experiment was followed up by another psychologist Fei Xu, again with 9-month-olds. She worked with two objects, say a toy duck and a toy ball, which she showed to the babies, before hiding both objects behind a screen. In one experimental condition, she accompanied each showing of an object with an utterance identifying its specific type, e.g. *Look, a duck* or *Look, a ball*. In the other condition, the utterance merely identified both objects as of the same generic type, e.g. *Look, a toy* (twice). When this was done, and both objects had been placed behind the screen, the screen was taken away, to reveal just one object (because one had been sneaked away), and the baby's reaction was watched. Babies looked longer, in apparent surprise at the appearance of only one object, in the condition when two different labels (*duck* and *ball*) had been used, than in the other condition when just one label (*toy*) had been used. The use of different labels affected the babies' expectations of what was behind the screen. They noticed that something was missing more often when it had been given a different label from the other thing.

The overt use of a word can draw attention to an aspect of a practical problem that might otherwise be overlooked. Psychologists Sam Glucksberg and Robert Weisberg set subjects a practical problem to solve using a shallow open box containing tacks. In one condition the box was labelled *box*, and in the other condition it was labelled *TACKS*. The practical solution to the problem involved using the box to catch some wax from a candle. Subjects hit upon this solution quicker when they saw the label *box* than when they saw the label *TACKS*. The overt use of a word drew the subjects' attention to the possible use of the object named. Again, simply knowing the words *left* and *right* enhances a child's ability to carry out a searching task, though the instructions given don't use these words, as psychologist

Linda Hermer-Vazquez and colleagues have shown. Children who had already learned these words were better searchers than children who hadn't, taking age into account.

Words in a public language act as a mental prop, helping us, and in harder cases even enabling us, to think more abstract thoughts. Some thought is possible without language, and languageless animals can think about things up to a point. Humans, with language, can think beyond that point. (Our thinking abilities are still bounded by working memory limits; we are not infinite calculating machines.) This suggests a co-evolutionary spiral between the rise of public language and the capacity for more complex thought. The facilitating effect of public words on abstract thought is another strong argument against the theoretical claim that language evolved as a purely internal private means of carrying out complex thought, unrelated to its public function of communication.

Not all prelinguistic concepts are affected by getting words for them. Concepts of basic emotional facial expressions such as anger and disgust are not affected by words, as psychologist Disa Sauter and her team have shown by studies with speakers of Yucatec Maya, a language that has no separate words for these emotions. Yet the Yucatec speakers make the same categorical distinctions between faces showing these emotions as do German speakers. In other cases, as we have seen above, even at the simple level of vocabulary, having a word for something may sometimes affect how we conceive of it. Originally private concepts, once attached to a public label used by other people, are no longer completely one's own. They become standardized and tweaked and refined in subtle ways. Concepts preceded words in evolution (as we saw in Chapter 4), and languageless animals are able to think in even some quite abstract ways about the world. But once words enter the scene, words and thoughts become intertwined. Universal emotions such as anger or disgust, and the conceptual recognition of these, including the facial expressions for them, are not affected by words, and there is good translatability between languages for these emotions. But other concepts are more specific to particular cultures, having been moulded by their languages, and there is only clumsy translatability between languages for such concepts. There is no exact German word for English *kindness*, and no exact Arabic word for English *interesting*. In particular contexts, one can find words that do the job acceptably, but the same word will not work properly in all the contexts in which the English words are used. Conversely, there are words in other cultures that have no exact equivalent in English.

7

Building powerful grammar engines

You may not admit it, but you know a tremendous lot of grammar. You must do, to understand the utterances in your native language buzzing around you, and to readily give back more of the same. OK, so you can't describe in technical terms, like *pronoun, adjective, participle*, what allows you to manage this complicated feat, but you do it unconsciously all the time. Think of the workings of grammar in your head as like the workings of your digestive system, complicated, and unconscious. In your head you have grammar, a complex repertoire of words and constructions and ways of combining them to express complex meanings. And the other folk around you have something very similar in their heads too, so that you can all 'sing from the same hymn sheet'. 'Twas not ever thus. Over time, maybe very short times, groups of cooperating individuals built up the grammars of their languages to incorporate all the intricacies that a learner must master if she is to function like a native.

What is 'syntax'?

Linguists call grammar 'syntax'. Syntax, in its simplest sense, is not necessarily connected with meaning. Any system with rules for combining elements has a syntax, but the elements need not mean anything or add up to anything meaningful. Among human activities, music has syntactic structure. To be a certain tune, it is not the absolute pitch of the notes that count, but the intervals between them.

You can pick out the *Ode to Joy*, or *Waltzing Matilda*, or any tune you like, on a piano starting with any key, white or black. A well-formed tune, in a particular musical tradition, has notes in relationships and an order sanctioned by the tradition. In this sense, music has syntax. Music is broadly meaningful, in that a tune, or even a phrase within a tune, may convey a particular emotion, such as sadness or wistfulness or lightheartedness. But the individual notes in a tune have no meanings, and do not contribute anything that can be found in the overall emotional meaning conveyed—music is not semantically compositional.

In language, the phonological structure of words also has syntactic structure, in this broad sense of 'syntactic', but is not semantically compositional. The phonemes that make up words don't have any individual meanings, and therefore don't contribute any meaning to a whole word. For example, the word *pet* is a sequence of three phonemes /p e t/. On its own /p/ doesn't mean anything, nor do /e/ or /t/. But there are rules of combination of phonemes (linguists call them 'phonotactic' rules); you can't string phonemes together in any conceivable order. Languages have syntactic structure at two levels, the phonological level (the 'phonotactics' of the language) and at the level of combining meaningful words and affixes, called the 'morphosyntax' of the language. Only the morphosyntactic level is semantically compositional.

Having syntactic structure at two levels, one semantically compositional and the other not, is a characteristic of all languages, and is called by linguists 'duality of patterning'. Given the way human memory and our vocal and auditory abilities are, it is functionally efficient to have these two levels of patterning. Our tongues can only consistently get around a limited inventory of separate speech sounds, and our ears can only detect acoustic distinctions down to a certain level of subtlety (as we saw in Chapter 5). So if we can put these sounds into memorized sequences, and have enough memory capacity to store thousands of such sequences (i.e. words), that is an efficient solution for the task of expressing vast numbers of meanings, given a semantically compositional syntax.

To have a syntax, a system of expressions must have a certain productivity. That is, the rules for combining the basic elements into strings must offer different options for plugging substrings into an overall string. Human languages are extremely productive. They have tens of thousands of meaningful elements, the words and affixes, and they combine these very freely (but not so unconstrainedly that 'anything goes'), so that in principle billions of different sentences are possible in a language, if you know its syntactic system.

The enormous syntactic productivity of languages is motivated by the usefulness of being able to communicate many things about the world, and in many different ways as suited to the relationships between speakers. This pervasive use of languages to convey meaning adds further complexities to their syntactic structure. Syntax is more than just putting things next to each other. The syntactic well-formedness of a word string can sometimes require that words quite far away from each other be matched in some specific way. Take for example the French sentence *La porte du jardin de mon oncle est ouverte* (lit. 'The door of the garden of my uncle is open'). Here the 'feminine' form of the adjective *ouverte* is grammatically required because of the 'feminine gender' of the noun *porte* seven words earlier. This has nothing to do with the meanings of the words or the whole sentence; it is a purely grammatical requirement. This example involved hierarchical structure, as much of the syntactic structure of human languages does. The subject phrase *La porte du jardin de mon oncle* is a grammatical chunk, which could have been longer or shorter (depending on what one wanted to say), but the dependency of the adjective at the end of the sentence would be the same, no matter how close or how far away it is from the 'agreeing' noun *porte*. A more comprehensive way of describing the same facts is to say that French has a 'predicate adjective' sentence construction, consisting of three parts: a noun phrase, then some agreeing form of the verb *être*, then the agreeing adjective. Mention here of a 'noun phrase' is a reference to another type of construction with specified parts, which in French typically include an article (such as *le, la, les, un,* or *une*), maybe some other stuff, and an obligatory noun. I've been deliberately vague here, not to bore you with details.

The point is that the syntax of human languages is best seen as putting 'constructions' together, sometimes side by side, but more often one inside another, and sometimes even interwoven in more intricate ways.

Now what, you will reasonably ask, is a 'construction'? The simplest constructions are single words. More complex constructions are composed of simpler constructions, down to the most basic level, that of words. And complex constructions have fillable slots in them reserved for plugging in other specified types of construction, as we just saw with the French example, where a noun phrase construction is slotted into the predicate adjective sentence construction. This hierarchical embedding of constructions within each other in human languages is almost entirely motivated by semantics, i.e. by matters of meaning. Sometimes we want to convey complex messages, which are best composed of smaller meaningful parts.

I mentioned the relationship of 'agreement' between the subject of a French sentence and a predicate adjective, where the two agreeing words can be quite far apart. This is a case of what linguists call 'long-distance dependencies'—a word in one part of a sentence relates in some systematic way to a word some distance away. Another kind of long-distance dependency arises when we shift information around in a sentence for the purposes of highlighting one part over others. Here is an English conversational example: *That busker on the High Street, Sue said she hadn't seen him around lately*. Here, the words *busker* and *him* refer to the same person. So there is a long-distance dependency between *busker* and *him* in this example. Long-distance dependencies of this kind are a unique characteristic of human languages. We are able to take in a string of words and hold some of them in working memory waiting to be 'resolved' by later incoming bits of the sentence. In more complex cases, the resolving parts of the sentence are not actual words but apparent gaps which can only be made sense of by assuming that some earlier word is understood as filling the gap. For example, the string *Sue said she saw* is not complete—something is missing after *saw*: saw what? or who? But in the question *Who did Sue say she saw?* we don't mind the gap, because we understand that the question word

Who at the beginning of the sentence relates to the verb *saw* as its object.

Did humans start by singing like birds?

The songs of many songbirds have syntax, but their overall meaning, either courtship or territory-claiming, is in no way a function of the meanings of the individual notes. The songs of some whales are also quite complex, and their 'meanings' seem to be indicators of identity, as a way of maintaining contact with others in the group. Again, despite the complex patterns of whale songs, the individual notes don't appear to mean anything that can be taken as contributing to the meaning of the whole, which says essentially 'This is me' or 'Here I am'.

One theory about the origin of syntactic organization in human languages is that originally humans (or their close ancestors) 'sang' like birds, for purposes of courtship, in songs that had, like birdsong and whale song, somewhat complex syntax (rules of combination of the elements) but no compositional semantics, i.e. the meaning of a song was not derived from the meanings of individual notes. Charles Darwin himself, along with Jean-Jacques Rousseau, believed in this idea. The route to human semantically compositional syntax, they thought, was via the marrying of meanings with the existing complex song. In this view, pure uninterpreted syntax came first, and then meanings were fitted onto it. The song-as-origin-of-syntax idea is that a semantically compositional language first came into existence through the notes getting associated with elements of meaning.

For birdlike song to be a suitable candidate for the basis of syntax in human language, it needs to have a structure that is suitable for marriage with compositional semantics. We'll look at some birdsong, and some whale song, to see what candidate structural elements it may have. The most notable relevant feature is some hierarchical phrasal structuring. The term 'phrase' is used here in the same sense as in music. In human languages, phrases are identified largely by appeal to meaning. For instances, noun phrases such as *the quick brown fox* pick out referent objects in the world. A meaningful phrase such as this is embedded in a sentence, giving a hierarchical part–whole structure. A typical simple sentence contains several noun phrases as members. Human sentences are organized with meaningful building blocks that are smaller than the whole but larger than the atomic elements, the words. These middle-sized chunks are phrases.

Birdsong and whale song also have phrases, but not (of course) identified semantically, in terms of their meanings, because they have no meanings. The phrases of birdsong and whale song stand out because they are often repeated in strict order at specific places in the song. Zebra finch song, for instance, uses phrases that the birdsong researchers call 'motifs'. A typical zebra finch motif consists of six different notes, always sung in exactly the same order, over and over again, up to about four times. This succession of motifs is obligatorily preceded by certain introductory notes and followed by certain other obligatory ending notes. Chaffinch song is similar, but more loosely organized than the extremely stereotyped zebra finch song. Chaffinch song also uses recognizable phrases. Some chaffinch songs repeat one phrase a few times, then move on to several repetitions of a different phrase, before ending with an obligatory final 'flourish'. Birdsong researchers use this terminology of phrasing and are agreed on the hierarchical structure of the songs. The songs of some whales, in particular humpback whales, are more complex. An individual humpback whale only sings one song, over and over, and each version may last as long as 20 minutes. Within the song there is clear phrasal organization, with one recognizable sequence being repeated many times before the whale switches to repetition of another sequence, then to repetition of a third distinct sequence of notes, and so on, with the whole song consisting of as many as six separate phrasal cycles.

So birdsong and whale song have phrases. If we are to push the Darwin/Rousseau idea to its detailed implications, early humans sang songs like birds or whales, with phrases, and these phrases somehow got taken up as suitable for association with the kind of middle-sized meanings that phrases in human languages can carry. It is not clear how the details can be worked out, as, beside the similarities, there are important differences between bird and whale phrasal structure and that of human languages. In birdsong, the depth of such hierarchical embedding of phrases within the song is limited to just one layer. There are not short phrases within medium-length phrases within long phrases (like this). In birdsong, identical phrases are usually repeated a number of times; indeed, this is what helps them to be identified as phrases. But this is not characteristic of human, meaning-carrying phrases. Birdsong has very limited productivity, compared to language. The champion songster is the nightingale, which can have up to 200 different songs. But the structure of even the nightingale songs is different from human song. Nightingale songs, and birdsong generally, does not reuse its resources at many different places in a song. A phrase that can appear in one song typically does not appear in (many) other songs. If an expert hears the last few notes of a nightingale song, for instance, she can predict what all the preceding notes in the song were. Try to guess the whole of any sentence in this book on just the basis of its final few words! A striking fact about birdsong generally is that the number of notes making up songs is greater than the number of songs. This is just the reverse of the productivity of human language, in which the number of words is always far less than the number of sentences that can be made from them. Humans are combinatorially promiscuous, whereas songbirds are not, to anything like the same degree.

Finally, our closest primate relatives don't sing. The closest singing relative is the gibbon, whose songs are not unlike some birdsong. I am generally sceptical of the song-as-origin-of-language story. But to give the idea its due, maybe the skill to command complex sequences was relevant. In a sense, the songbirds and singing whales are a mirror image of some aphasic patients, who have complex thoughts like healthy people but can't organize grammatical sequences of words expressing these thoughts. Birds can organize their outpourings hierarchically, into phrases, but don't have anything detailed to say, except broad courtship, territorial, or identity-marking messages. But just possibly, if only they could conceive complex propositional meanings, and desire to communicate them, they could adapt their songs to this purpose.

Birdsong does show a feature of songbird lives in which they are much more than the simple stimulus–response machines they are often taken to be. Speakers of human languages are routinely said to have a mental grammar in their heads that determines the regular forms in which they express themselves, called a person's 'grammatical competence' by linguists. Your grammatical competence sits permanently in your brain, whether you are asleep or awake, or actually using language at the time or not. It is clear that songbirds too have permanent representations in their brains of the patterns of their complex songs. This shows in a remarkable way. When a songbird chick hears its parent singing, it does not respond. Birds and their chicks don't begin to have meaningful conversations like human parents and children. The young songbird at this stage is completely passive. But something important is happening in its brain, because, as much as six months later, when its parent is long gone, it starts to try to sing. At first, it makes sounds that are unlike the parent's song it heard months before. Over a few weeks, it practises and its performance gradually improves and finally it ends up singing like a recognizable songster of its species. All that time, apparently, some pattern of the right song to sing has been registered in its brain, and it tries over a period of a few weeks to get it right, in a process called 'subsong', which has been likened to the babbling of human babies. The important point here is that humans and songbirds are alike in having both complex behaviour and internal mental representations guiding that behaviour. Sure, we humans are the only creatures who can introspect and theorize about our own internal representations, but that is another matter.

Packaging messages in clauses and sentences

Symbol-trained chimpanzees like Panzee and Nim can come out with strings of meaningful elements (Panzee using a lexigram board and Nim using American Sign Language). One of Panzee's was *hide, stick, hide, stick, stick, stick, hide, kiwi, kiwi*; one of Nim's was *hug Nim hug*. In a trivial sense, these utterances are semantically compositional. The overall meaning of Panzee's utterance, for example, was something to do with a kiwi fruit, a stick, and hiding; it wasn't to do with an apple, or a stone, or showing. That's why she picked those signs, and strung them together. The context was enough for a receiver to figure out that she wanted him to poke about with a stick and find a hidden kiwi fruit. This is trivial compositionality, not making use of any specific method of stringing the signs together. Trivial compositionality naturally arises the moment two or more meaningful 'words' are strung together. Most likely, such trivial compositionality preceded more complex forms of compositionality, assisted by grammatical markers, and the grammatical markers arose later.

Such simple forms of language do exist in humans today, in the productions of toddlers, aphasics, and speakers of pidgin 'languages' who communicate in improvised ways using just content words. Here are some examples: *goat try eat lid*, spoken by a two-year-old; *wife, Rosa ... uh ... take ... uh ... love ... uh ... ladies ... uh Ocean uh hospital*, by an aphasic patient; *you me downtown movie fun* signed in an improvised pidgin by a deaf teenager asking a girl for a date. These are examples labelled as modern cases of protolanguage, productions by modern speakers in exceptional circumstances, lacking little grammatical marker words. Such productions plausibly illustrate what early language would have been like.

A machine or animal that just spewed out words one after the other, like Panzee or Nim, is missing a fundamental feature of language: its structuring into packages with clear beginnings and ends, i.e. sentences. Simple sentences consist of a single clause, such as *John gave Mary a book*. More complex sentences consist of several clauses, for example *When she came home, John told Mary that the child she had met had measles*. This last sentence contains three subordinate clauses, underlined here, and one of them is inside another. A good rule of thumb is 'one main verb per clause'.

The grammatical system of a language dictates no limit to the size of sentences, measured in number of clauses, though in practice working memory constrains the length of sentences in use. But grammatical systems do constrain the size of individual clauses. A clause has a main verb and between one and three 'arguments' of the verb. Verb arguments are usually noun phrases and play the roles of subject, object, and indirect object; we just saw this in *John gave Mary a book*. Each verb specifies how many of such arguments it can take. Intransitive verbs, like *sleep*, take only one argument, a subject; transitive verbs, like *see*, take two arguments, a subject and a direct object; and ditransitive verbs like *give* take three arguments, a subject, a direct object, and an indirect object. That's it. There are odd examples in some languages for which it can be claimed that a basic clause contains more than these canonical three arguments, but such cases are debatable and rare. Note that the verb's arguments themselves can be lengthened ad lib, for example by using many adjectives modifying the head noun of the argument. But the number of a verb's possible arguments in a clause is definitely limited. The clear preference for one to three verb arguments, and no more, that we find in all languages is something to be explained. And moreover there is an evolutionary explanation for it—here it is.

Clauses describe events or states of affairs, involving some participants. The participants are typically objects (which may be people), as in John giving Mary a book, an event involving three participant objects. Independently of linguistics, psychologists have discovered a clear limit to the number of objects that the visual system can track at a time. The typical limit is four objects, with variation depending on individuals and tasks. The magical number 4, as it has been labelled, is also argued by psychologist Nelson Cowan to be the rough limit of human short-term memory (not 7, as earlier claimed by George Miller). And 4 is the typical limit for 'subitizing', the judging of how many items are in an array seen at a quick glance, without counting. Roughly the same low working limit of about four or five objects has also been detected in chimpanzees and macaques, and so is likely to be much more ancient than language itself. In surveying the world around us we take in a scene, perhaps analyse it, and then move on to taking in another scene. The number of tracked participants is limited to no more than four. The term 'minimal subscene' has been used to describe these small packages of our ongoing experience. Briefly taking in a static scene containing many details that one might at greater leisure pore over, the eyes typically flit between a very small number of locations in the scene, seldom more than four. Quickly looking at a face, eye-tracking shows that our gaze is directed at no more than four areas: the eyes, the mouth, and the nose. The world itself is not packaged. The human perceptual apparatus packages the world into small units with up to four participants. This aspect of our perception of the world is quite ancient, as apes and monkeys seem to work in the same way. The clausal organization of languages reflects a norm comfortably within this ancient limit on perceptual structure. Acknowledging this influence of the perceptual system on language structure avoids the vicious circularity implicit in the traditional definition of a sentence as the expression of 'a complete thought'.

In the emergence of Nicaraguan Sign Language, there was a stage when sentences were limited to describing events with just a single participant. In one experiment, children at an early stage in the evolution of the language were shown a video of a man pushing a woman over, and asked to describe it in signs. At this stage, what typically emerged was a two-package description, separated by a pause or a lowering of the hands. Thus a child would sign MAN PUSH, then pause briefly before signing WOMAN FALL, simplifying the event into two phases. This is not to suggest that the children could not take in an event with more than one participant. Rather, at the early rudimentary stage that the language had reached at that time, the only assured conventional means of expressing this event was to separate it into a two-package message. Later in the evolution of NSL, children squashed these two phases together, first typically as MAN WOMAN PUSH-FALL, and often later as MAN PUSH-FALL WOMAN. Thus in the evolution of this language a sequence of increasing grammatical package size was observed, as the conventions shared by the signing group gradually became more complex and able to handle larger packages.

It seems likely that some such progression also occurred in the evolution of the very earliest human languages, from simple clauses naming one participant to somewhat more complex clauses naming several participants. Perhaps it happened very fast, maybe over the course of just a few generations. The speed of the expansion would depend on factors such as the size of the social group and the frequency of communicative utterances among them. We know these factors affect the spread of conventions. In a small group of taciturn individuals not given to saying much to each other, such conventions would spread more slowly, if at all. Early humans at the vital stage when conventional languages were taking off were probably about as inclined to try to talk to each other as modern humans. However, the natural limit of grammatical package size did not expand beyond the size of a perceptual minimal scene, namely with up to four participants. I emphasize that this limit is the size limit of simple sentences, consisting of one clause, the basic package of human syntax. Modern languages can form more complex sentences by conjoining clauses or embedding clauses one inside the other, up to some practical limit imposed by the working memory involved in processing sentences.

The most elementary way to combine clauses is by mere juxtaposition. Children in the early cohort at the Managua deaf school combined MAN PUSH with WOMAN FALL, as we have seen, albeit with a pause between the clauses. Julius Caesar reputedly used simple juxtaposition of clauses in his *veni, vidi, vici* report of a successful campaign. This is three one-word Latin clauses juxtaposed to make a sentence. Clauses in many languages cannot usually be as terse as Caesar's Latin, and the English translation of his example ('I came, I saw, I conquered') is also a juxtaposition of three clauses to make a sentence. It is a small step from juxtaposition of clauses to marking the fact of an intended relation between the two clauses by some overt coordinating conjunction, such as English *and*. Some striking literary narratives take this simple form, as in:

In the beginning God created the heaven and the earth.
And the earth was without form, and void;
and darkness was upon the face of the deep.
And the Spirit of God moved upon the face of the waters.

If the occurrences of *and* were stripped out of this text, it would be harder to interpret where one clause ends and the next begins.

It is a greater step, and one needing more complex processing powers, to embed one clause inside another. The fact that one clause is embedded inside another is typically marked by what linguists call a 'subordinating conjunction' such as English *that*, *if*, or *because*. Languages adopt subordination of clauses historically later than coordination with words like *and*. Many languages make very sparse use of clause subordination, while making much freer use of clause conjoining. We can extrapolate that the earliest languages had only juxtaposition of clauses, then developed markers of coordination of clauses (like *and*), and only later, perhaps much later, developed ways of signalling that one clause was intended to be understood as playing a role inside the interpretation of another, i.e. marking subordination of clauses.

To give an example of how the development from juxtaposition to subordination could plausibly have happened (and foreshadowing the topic of the next section), consider the dual use in English of the word *that*. *That* can be used as a pronoun referring to some thing, action, or event, as in *I saw that*. Still as a pronoun, it can naturally be used in a 'topicalized' position, as in *That I saw*. Now imagine this last sentence juxtaposed after, e.g. *There's the house*, giving *There's the house. That I saw* (where the punctuation represents a spoken pause or shift in intonation). It is a small step from this to a fluent two-clause sentence *There's the house that I saw* with no pause or intonation shift. Such a story accounts for the fact that English *that* now serves several different purposes, as a demonstrative pronoun and also a subordination marker, of a relative clause.

Making grammar

No existing language of a community is entirely without grammar. But some have more grammar than others. There are different ways in which grammar can be complex. I will mention two prominent dimensions, and then use them to speculate about what the very earliest languages, in which grammar was just beginning to emerge, would have been like. These dimensions are (1) fineness of classification and subclassification of words into types like the classical parts of speech, and (2) degree of inflectedness of words, called 'morphological complexity' by linguists. Actually these two dimensions are intertwined, as we will see. We will start with the classification of how words fit into the grammar of a language, describing the present state of affairs in some languages, and applying what is known about how they got to be that way.

Noun and verb are the basic major word classes, or syntactic categories, as linguists call them, in any language. Some languages get close to making no distinction between nouns and verbs, while in other languages the distinction is clearly visible in the positions that words occupy in sentences. In this dimension too, some languages have more grammar than others. How did this most basic grammatical distinction evolve? The answer lies in the central special function of communication in language: giving information about identified objects. One bit of the signal identifies the topic talked about, and another part gives information about it. *That's wrong*, you may say; in doing so, you have illustrated the idea. The word *that* points to something in the context, without describing it, and *wrong* says something about it. Where the thing talked about cannot be guessed from context, a definite descriptive expression can be used, as in *Jim's theory is wrong*. Here, something is identified by a noun phrase, *Jim's theory*, and it is asserted that it is wrong. As linguists put it, the noun phrase here is the 'Topic' of the sentence, and the verb phrase *is wrong* is the 'Comment'. In Aristotle's influential analysis of thought and grammar, these terms are paralleled by 'subject' and 'predicate'. In the most ordinary kind of simple sentence, the subject expression, with a noun at its core, is the Topic, and the predicate expression, with a verb at its core, is the Comment. This is the original basis for the pervasive noun/verb distinction at the heart of the grammar of languages. As languages have evolved to allow more complex sentence structures, the simple correlation of nouns with Topics and subjects, and of verbs with Comments and predicates, has in some cases been overlaid. For instance, in the sentence *Mary,*

John didn't invite, used in contextually rather unusual circumstances, the subject of the verb, *John,* is not actually the Topic of the sentence, which is *Mary.* Nevertheless, it is possible to see such sentences as transformations, for unusual conversational purposes, of the basic Subject–Predicate structure, in which something is identified by a noun, and something is said about it by a verb expression.

In modern languages, the most common position for the verb in a sentence is near the end, after its subject and object. Classical Latin was like this, with e.g. *Brutus Caesarem occisit,* literally 'Brutus Caesar killed'. Linguists call this word order 'SOV'. English, with its Subject–Verb–Object preferred order, is called 'SVO', and Welsh, which puts the verb at the beginning of a sentence, is a 'VSO' language. Languages can change their preferred word orders, but there is no known case of a language changing to SOV; any attested historical change is away from SOV, leading to the hypothesis that the earliest languages were SOV, putting the verb at the end of the sentence. In modern times, we see newly invented sign languages also starting off with SOV word order.

All languages make some distinction between 'content words' and 'function words'. Content words carry descriptive meaning; nouns, verbs, adjectives, and adverbs are types of content word. Function words are typically little words, and they signal relations between parts of sentences, or something about the pragmatic import of a sentence, e.g. whether it is a question. Lewis Carroll's 'Jabberwocky' poem illustrates the distinction well;

Twas brillig, and the slithy toves
Did gyre and gimble in the wabe,
All mimsy were the borogoves,
And the mome raths outgrabe.

In this poem, all the made-up words are content words; all the others are function words. In English, function words include determiners, such as *the, a, my, your,* pronouns (e.g. *I, me, you, she, them*), various auxiliary verbs (e.g. *have, is, can, will, do*), coordinating conjunctions (*and, or, but*) and subordinating conjunctions (e.g. *if, when, as, because*). Prepositions are a borderline case. They have some semantic content, but are a small closed class, allowing hardly any historical innovation. Some English prepositions serve a mainly grammatical function, like *of* (what is the meaning of *of*?) and others have clear descriptive (and relational) content, like *under*. New content words in a language can be readily invented; new nouns, in particular, are continually being coined, and new verbs (e.g. *Google*, *gazump*) and adjectives (e.g. *naff*, *grungy*) also not infrequently come into use. The small set of function words in a language, by contrast, is much more fixed, and relatively steady over centuries. Function words tend, across languages, to be short, unstressed in the stream of speech, and very frequent in texts, and they have relatively simpler phonological structure than content words. The disjointed speech of patients with Broca's aphasia typically omits function words, or any other signal of grammatical structure. There is psycholinguistic evidence that function words are recognized faster in listening to speech than content words, and with less possibility of being mistaken for other words.

We have already seen how conjunctions such as English *and* mark the boundaries of clauses strung together, introducing some clarity that would be missing if clauses were simply juxtaposed with no grammatical markers. Despite the relative fixedness of function words at any stage in a language's history, in the long-term perspective of language evolution, we can trace their original emergence in languages. They are historically derived from content words by a process of 'grammaticalization'. This family of mechanisms provides the central route by which languages become grammatically more complex. The relevant biological features of human beings, through which these mechanisms operate, have remained constant over the historical period in which grammaticalization works, of course. So grammaticalization is not part of the specifically biological history of our species. The term 'grammaticalization' is attributed to the French linguist Antoine Meillet, a pioneer in this area. The term is apt, because it is a process by which a language becomes more grammatically organized, i.e. comes to have a greater number of particular rules applying to specific subclasses of words, such as function words. I will mention some well-attested examples.

Auxiliary verbs are often historically traceable to main verbs, i.e. to verbs with the same distributional privileges as other content verbs. English *have* is still used as a main verb, denoting possession, as in *I have a book*, but has also become specialized as a function word indicating recent relevant pastness, as in *I have caught a fish*. In this use, *have* is closely restricted to occurring with the past participle of another verb, like *caught* in this example. *Have* has also been grammaticalized in a different way in English, to indicate obligation, as in *I have to go*, to which a special rule of devoicing can apply as in *hafta*. Another auxiliary verb historically descended from a content word is the English modal verb *can*, as in *Can you swim?*, derived from the Old English *cunnan* 'know, be acquainted with'. Similarly, the English modal verb *will* signifying future time, is derived from Old English *willan* 'want to'. The Spanish auxiliary *estar* is derived from the Latin main verb *stare* 'to stand'. A similar process of creating copular verbs (like English *be*) from verbs denoting ways of standing or sitting is reported for Australian languages. A language with few or no auxiliary verbs is less grammaticalized (one can say 'has less grammar' in this respect) than one with more auxiliary verbs.

English has prepositions, placed before a noun. Some other languages have 'postpositions', doing the same kind of work as prepositions, but placed after the noun, as in Hungarian *a posta mellett* 'beside the post office'. In English, *ago* is a rare case of a postposition. Across languages, these words can often be seen to be historically derived from either nouns or verbs (both pathways occur). A currently ongoing example is the use of *come* in *come Christmas*, meaning the same as *by Christmas*. In Ewe, a language of Ghana, a preposition meaning 'from' has been adapted from a verb meaning 'to come from'. A case of a preposition derived from a noun is found in Icelandic *bak(i)* 'behind', which comes from the body-part noun meaning 'a person's back'. The Hungarian postposition *mellett* 'beside' comes from the noun *mell* 'breast'.

Those were examples of function words being historically derived from content words. There are also cases of historical movement within the overall class of function words. Historically, some function words are more basic than others. Definite articles are often derived from demonstrative pronouns. French *le* and *la* come from Latin demonstratives *ille* and *illa*. This historical process has left a residue in the modern language, as *le* and *la* are also used as object pronouns, as in *Je le vois* 'I see it'. Examples of the same 'demonstrative → definite article' shift can also be cited from English, German, and Hindi, among many other languages. Demonstrative pronouns like English *that*, as in *That's mine!*, can also give rise to subordinating conjunctions, as in *I know that he's coming* and *The man that I saw is here*. A similar development is clear in German, where *dass* is historically derived from *das*. Other subordinators, like English *which* and *who* (as in *the one who's coming*) are derived from question particles, still recognizable in *Who's coming?*. The same correspondence can be seen in French. A very common source of indefinite articles is the word for the numeral for 1. A modern correspondence is clearly seen in French *un* and German *ein*; in modern English such an obvious correspondence has been lost, but *an* is historically related to *one*.

Among content words, some languages do not distinguish a class of adjectives. To express something like 'a tall man', these languages often use some gerund-like form of a verb meaning 'to be tall'. A grammaticalization process can also mediate between different classes of content word. Swahili has formed adjectives meaning 'male' and 'female' from nouns meaning 'man' and 'woman'. In my lifetime, I have noted the word *fun* being stretched from use as a noun to use as an adjective, as in *They are fun people*.

The grammaticalization processes surveyed above are overwhelmingly unidirectional, from content word to function word. One seldom (many experts say never) finds a reverse case of a function word transmuting into a content word. Possible exceptions are when one talks of *ifs and buts*, meaning something like 'conditions and reservations'. But even this possibility does not deny that *if* and *but* were not themselves, way back in time, derived from content words. Indeed, one account of the origin of modern English *if* is that it is derived from an old Germanic word meaning 'doubt'. The strongly dominant unidirectionality of the content word → function word process means that we can project back to an early stage of languages in which there were no function words at all.

This brings us to the other dimension along which languages vary in complexity: the richness of their systems of word inflections. Inflections are systematic variations in the shape of words. Most inflections give semantic information. For instance, the endings on the German verb forms *komme, kommst, kommt, kommen* give information about the person and number of the subject of the verb, i.e. whether it's me, you, or some other person(s). English is less complex in this regard, having only two corresponding forms, *come* and *comes*. Semantic information about the time of an event is also conveyed by tense inflections, as in the differences between French *porte, porta, portait, portera,* and *porterait* 'carries, carried, was carrying, will carry, would carry'. Again, notice how English is simple by comparison, having only two ways of indicating time by word inflections. English speakers can express the same range of meaning as French speakers, but they don't do it so much using word inflections. German and French are not spectacular examples of highly inflected languages. Russian and Latin are more inflected, and we find highly inflected languages in many parts of the world, such as Shona, the main language of Zimbabwe, Pirahã, an Amazonian language, and Warlpiri, an Australian language. Hungarian and Finnish have over a dozen different case endings on nouns, some indicating the grammatical role of the noun in a sentence (e.g. subject or object), and some indicating spatial relations that in English are rendered by prepositions such as *in, on,* and *at*. Bantu languages of Africa have up to ten different classes of noun, each of which inflects for singular/plural in a different way. One more thing about inflections: they don't have to be suffixes, stuck onto the ends of words. They can be prefixes, like Russian markers of the aspect of a verb (e.g. marking the difference between the beginning of an action, or a continuing state, or a completed action), or Shona singular/plural markers (e.g. *muana* 'a child', *vana* 'children'). Inflection can also take the form of a change in the middle of a word, as in English strong verb alternations like *drive/drove/driven, swim/swam/swum, begin/began/begun*. More complicatedly, and less often, inflections can be complex templates around which the consonants of a word are fitted. Arabic has a lot of such template word inflection, as in *katab* 'he wrote', *tiktibi* 'you (feminine) are to write', *biyiktibu* 'they are writing', *haktib* 'I will write', *maktuub* 'written', *kaatib* 'writer', *maktab* 'writing place (desk)', and much more. It is fair to call this complex, even though all the same semantic distinctions can be made in English. English speakers just don't do it using inflections. We use strings of separate words, as in the translations just given. This is simpler in some sense, and definitely less compact.

At the opposite end of the scale of word-formation complexity are so-called 'isolating' languages. An extreme case of an isolating language has no word inflections at all. The various Chinese languages, including Mandarin and Cantonese, get close to having no word inflections, as do Vietnamese and Indonesian. English is near the isolating end of the scale, not having much word inflection. Languages with little word inflection tend to be stricter in their word order. If the grammatical role (subject or object) of a word is indicated by an inflection, it can float about to many different parts of a sentence, as in Latin, but in isolating languages this would lead to undesirable ambiguity.

There is a two-part evolutionary issue here. How do affixes on words arise? And why do some languages have them while others don't? The answers to both questions involve the social circumstances in which the language is used, and reveal an interesting turnabout in the history of morphological complexity over the ages. We will start with what is known about the origins of word inflections.

For inflections in some languages, there is available historical evidence that they were once isolated words, able to stand on their own, and have been squashed into the neighbouring words, losing their capacity for independent phonetic stress, for instance. In several Romance languages, including French and Spanish, the inflections marking future tense are derived from a once independent word meaning 'to have'. For example, original Latin *cantare habemus*, literally 'to sing we have', got squashed into one word *cantarabemus*, eventually becoming modern Spanish *cantaremos* 'we will sing'. Another example, deeper in time, and so somewhat more debatable, is the origin of the English past tense marker -*ed*, which is believed to have come from a once independent verb meaning 'did'. Roughly, back in the distant past of Germanic languages, something equivalent to *talk did* becoming *talked* happened, it is supposed. In French, adding the suffix *-ment* to *heureuse* 'happy' gives *heureusement* 'happily', and this process of making an adverb out of an adjective is very productive. This suffix *-ment* (*-mente* in Italian) is historically derived from a once freestanding Latin word *mentis* 'mind'. Very similarly the English suffix *-ly*, which also converts an adjective into an adverb, is historically derived from an ancient Germanic word meaning 'body', akin to modern German *Leiche* 'corpse'.

We have seen a two-stage grammaticalization process, from content words to function words and from function words to inflections. These steps are unidirectional. There is no going back, so it is very plausible that the earliest languages had no function words and no inflections. Thus the earliest languages would have been like toddler-speak, e.g. *goat try eat lid*, or modern pidgins, e.g *You me downtown movie fun*.

Grammaticalization is not an abstract force working on languages. There are various mechanisms, different in detail. They all have in common an influence of frequent production on memorized convention. Combinations of words used very frequently get routinized and become phonetically slurred. A Spanish child hearing a fast spoken version of *cantare habemus* (the 'h' is anyway silent in Spanish) could well hear it as a single word *cantaremos*, unconsciously draw the conclusion that this is how future time is expressed, and generalize the principle to other verbs. The process involves adult shortcuts reinterpreted as convention by children. We will see the same general process in the evolution of sound systems in Chapter 8.

Civilization and grammar

For most of our existence, humans lived in small isolated traditional communities. The very recent rise of civilization has influenced the history of languages in different directions. On the one hand, increased cooperative contact between people speaking diverse languages has tended to simplify grammar. On the other, the invention of writing has allowed for the use of more complicated grammar, at least in quantitative terms. I'll discuss these developments in turn.

In the hunter-gatherer groups in which humans have lived for most of the past 200,000 years, group identity was a force for social cohesion, in competition with other groups. What little contact there was between tribes or bands was often hostile. People lived in small geographically isolated communities. Any exogamy was likely to be with near neighbours, who spoke a similar language. Children were raised with little contact with outsiders. There was little or no motivation to communicate with outsiders. Hence the languages of such small groups were free to evolve in their own idiosyncratic ways, uninfluenced by other languages. There is a robust negative statistical correlation between the morphological complexity of a language and the size of the population that speaks it. That is, smaller groups tend to speak languages with richer systems of word inflection. We know that grammaticalization produces morphological complexity, and we can easily envisage the forces of grammaticalization working undisturbed over long periods of time to produce rich inflectional systems in small geographically isolated groups.

Nineteenth-century historical linguists tended to paint a picture of a Golden Age of language structure, exemplified by the Classical languages, Ancient Greek, Sanskrit, and Latin, in which languages were 'perfect', meaning that they had rich systems of inflections. After that, it was all apparently downhill, with modern languages tending to lose this perfection. No good explanation was given for this apparent decline. Whatever factors had produced the rich inflectional systems of classical languages were not identified, and it was not clear why the evolution of languages should have turned in a different direction, degenerating in the common view, in recent historical times. Now we can see an answer.

Only in the very recent past, with the rise of cities, states, empires and long-distance trade, has contact between people speaking different languages had any influence on the languages themselves. Adults are not such faithful language learners as children, and their motivation tends to be different. Children learn to fit in with their community, replicating in themselves the complexities of the language spoken by the adults around them. Adults are concerned to be able to communicate, and so long as they can get a message across, however oddly, they satisfy their primary goal. Contact between adults speaking different languages tends to produce varieties of language in which morphological complexity is stripped out. Turkish immigrants into Germany, for instance, often simplify the system of German cases and genders, sometimes in effect reducing all nouns to a single case (instead of the proper German nominative, accusative, genitive, dative) and a single gender (instead of the proper German masculine, feminine, neuter). Languages with a history of external contact tend to have simpler morphology. One example involves a comparison between Norwegian and Faroese. Both languages are historically derived from a common North Germanic ancestor language. The Faroe islands have been relatively isolated during their history, while Norway has been subject to much more contact with outside world. As expected, Faroese preserves a more complex system of cases and genders, much of which has been lost in Norwegian. Modern English, emerging from contact between Norman French and Anglo-Saxon, has lost all the morphological complexity of Anglo-Saxon.

With the invention of writing and its gradual evolution into more and more tractable forms, starting in Sumer only about 5,000 years ago, grammar in use could become more complex. Modern written language has more complex grammar than spoken language, but only in a quantitative sense. Almost entirely, writing uses the same constructions as spoken language, but pushes their combination further and to greater depths of embedding. While spoken language rarely has one subordinate clause inside another, this is more often found in writing. And styles of writing differ in how far they push the combinatory possibilities. The language that is used by philosophers who have been trained in countries where Latin is taught in schools tends to be more complex. There, in case you hadn't noticed, that last sentence that you just read was an example of several subordinate clauses in one sentence, as is this present one. People in normal everyday life don't talk so complexly. Using several separate sentences instead of one complex one is more the norm. In formal situations like media interviews with politicians or cultural critics, spoken language takes more of a cue from written language, and people 'talk like a book'. There are a small number of phrases and idiomatic expressions that are only found in writing, such as the *Yours sincerely* at the end of a letter. Advanced written language is quite artificial, needing deliberate instruction in matters such as punctuation, paragraph structure, and choice of vocabulary. Not everybody manages it, so this degree of complexity is not part of a universal facile capacity for language. The written medium allows more complexity because the words on a page don't die on the air like speech, but can be re-scanned until you figure out what the writer intended.

8

Pronunciation gets complex

In Chapter 5 we saw the evolved characteristic abilities of humans in speaking and hearing. These traits are found in all (non-pathological) humans everywhere. In this chapter we will see how different cultural groups have picked up this biologically given ball and run with it, to arrive at quite diverse ways of putting their phonetic abilities to use.

Different languages have different ways of organizing their pronunciation. To a linguist, these are their 'phonological systems'. Languages pick different subsets of the available sounds of speech to make meaningful contrastive units ('phonemes'), they arrange them differently within words, and they modify them differently according to context. Some phonological systems are relatively simple, and some are more complex. How and why did languages get to have the various phonological systems they have? How did they get so organized, and why are some patterns of phonological organization more common than others in the world's languages, while some patterns don't occur at all?

The earliest vowel and consonant systems

The emergence of syllables makes the first big division of speech sounds, between vowels and consonants. Apart from a tiny number of exceptions in a few unusual languages, every syllable has at least one vowel, and it is typically flanked by consonants. Vowels contrast distinctively with consonants in the chain of speech. But along the axis of choice, vowels contrast distinctively only with other vowels, and likewise consonants only with other consonants. You can't, generally speaking, replace a vowel with a consonant or vice versa, to change one word into another. Thus, languages have two relatively self-contained subparts of their phonological systems, the vowel system and the consonant system. How do the internal details of vowel and consonant systems evolve?

We'll start with vowels. Don't be tempted to think there are only five vowels just because our Roman alphabet has the five 'vowel letters', i, e, a, o, and u. Spoken Ancient Latin happened to use just five vowels distinctively (albeit with long and short versions of each), and the writing system efficiently reflected the Romans' speech. The range of possible spoken vowels is continuous, like the colour spectrum. Just as you can't sensibly ask, 'How many colours are there?', you can't enumerate the number of possible spoken vowels. Each language carves up the vowel space in its own way. The most common partition of the space is a five-vowel system, like Latin. Many languages make more vowel distinctions, and some languages make fewer.

How many different vowels does English have? Well, it depends on your dialect. Standard American English makes fewer vowel distinctions than Standard Southern British English. For instance, many Southern British English speakers make a three-way distinction between *merry*, *marry*, and *Mary*, whereas for most Americans these all sound the same. Likewise, I pronounce *cot* and *caught*, and *coral* and *choral*, differently, but for most Americans these word pairs are spoken identically. In my accent of English, each of the following words is spoken with a different vowel: *pit, pet, pat, putt, put, pot, peat, pa, bought, boot, pate, bite, quoit, pout*. That's fourteen different vowels. Some English accents use fewer than this, and a few dialects use even more. English, of whatever dialect, is rather extravagant in the vowels it uses. Keeping them all separate is helped considerably by using different features of the possibilities afforded.

How did languages get their various vowel systems? Computer scientist and phonetician Bart de Boer has provided a very plausible answer, backed up by detailed computer simulations. I won't go into the finer points, but give a rough summary. In brief, de Boer envisages a population of agents who send each other vowel signals and try to recognize what they hear by relating it to vowels that they already know. After many exchanges, the agents' vowel inventories end up being adjusted so that all the agents in a simulation have similar sets of vowels. Some original vowels have dropped out, from lack of successful use, and occasionally a randomly introduced new vowel gets lucky and finds a niche in the vowel space where it is sufficiently distinct from others not to be confused with any of them. The model is one in which the vowel systems that emerge are selected, over many simulated exchanges between imagined users, on the basis how they provide a manageable number of vowels workably distinct from each other. Out of initial chaos, with no shared vowel system, the simulated populations gradually evolve toward the kind of system that can be found in real languages. De Boer ran his simulations many times. Because of the randomness involved in the initial sets of vowels and interfering random noise in the system, he got a range of different emergent vowel systems. Most often, he got a five-vowel system, like Latin, with the vowels roughly like [i, e, a, o, u]. Occasionally he got a four-vowel system, again with the vowels spread fairly equally into the corners of the vowel space. Sometime he even got a three-vowel system, with the same kind of 'triangular' set of vowels [i, a, u] as can be found in some languages. The simulations also sometimes yielded six-, seven-, and eight-vowel systems, always with the vowels spread around the possible space so that vowels were all about the same distance away from their nearest neighbours, and quite near the edges of the space. Most impressively, the frequency distribution of these different vowel systems was roughly (but not perfectly) parallel to the actual distributions of vowel systems across the languages of the world.

Economy and distinctiveness are the key drivers of the evolution of vowel systems. De Boer was following in the footsteps of eminent phoneticians (e.g. Ian Maddieson and Björn Lindblom) who have for many years emphasized the explanatory power of a balance between ease of articulation and distinctiveness. Such explanations are rooted in the concrete physical nature of the shape and musculature of the vocal tract, and the acoustics of the sounds it can make. Languages find a balance between maximum perceptual distinctiveness and minimum articulatory cost. Children learning a language are flexible and can pick up the vowel system of a community provided that the distinctions between vowels are not too fine or subtle. Where distinctions are quite subtle, as with *cot* and *caught*, they tend to get lost in the history of the dialect. This happened in Standard American English, whose modern speakers don't distinguish between *cot* and *caught*. Of course, speakers do all this adjustment of their speech mostly unconsciously. Depending on age and personality, people end up talking like the people around them, often without conscious effort. The evolution of vowel systems is thus a case of 'self-organization'. A system evolves not through any deliberate planning, but through the accumulation over time of a myriad of little adjustments by individuals responding to immediate pressures.

To our question 'How did languages get their various vowel systems?', this kind of answer is a functional and cultural one. Languages get vowel systems which facilitate communication. And language users in the same community adjust their behaviour, in this case their vowel systems, in response to interactions with other users, and the adjusted behaviour is transmitted, and perhaps readjusted, over many communicative episodes. It is an entirely plausible answer to the question. The acoustic/articulatory space in which this all happens is, of course, dictated by the genes that build the vocal tract and hearing mechanisms. But the genes allow a lot of freedom for different systems to evolve, and they do, but always guided by the prime functional considerations of economy ('don't have more vowels than you can realistically keep apart') and distinctiveness ('make sure your vowels are different enough from each other to be usable in conveying distinctions of meaning').

As with all computer modelling, de Boer's model is less complex than what can be found in real languages. The simulations don't take vowel length into account, or voice quality or tone. Phonetician Bert Remijsen has highlighted how Dinka, a Sudanese language with an unusually complex vowel system, distinguishes vowels not just by tongue position, but also by length (three ways), the relative creakiness of the vowel, and tone, but such cases are rare among the languages of the world. A more complex computer model could allow for these rarer possibilities, and it is likely that the same functional and cultural pressures could occasionally give rise to even such a rare kind of system as Dinka.

The factor of articulatory difficulty plays a role in explaining why systems like Dinka's are rare. All these dimensions of contrast are difficult to learn and control. Building on pioneering work by Ian Maddieson, phonetician Jean-Luc Schwartz and his colleagues have surveyed the types of vowel systems found across the world. They distinguish between a 'primary' type of vowel system, which exploits the more easily controlled parameters, such as front vowels with spread lips and back vowels with rounded lips, all oral (i.e. not nasalized), and without the complication of length contrasts. When a language has begun to exploit all of this primary vowel space, it may move to use 'secondary' features, such as nasalization, length contrasts, and less common combinations of tongue and lip position.

It seems reasonable to speculate that the vowel systems of the very earliest languages were simple, with probably no more than three vowels, and these were likely to have been like [i], [a], and [u]. In later phases of their evolution, languages would have continued to fill out the primary vowel space. Only in later stages would languages have started to venture into the secondary vowel space. Complications such as those found in Dinka, being harder to control in production and to distinguish in hearing, are characteristic of more mature developed languages, after long periods of phonological evolution.

Particular vowels emerge as targets that speakers aim for in speaking and seek to identify when listening. They emerge in the context of the parallel rise of other vowels concurrently emerging. Each vowel is sensitive to the presence of the others in the system, keeping as far as possible from them. Thus the system evolves as a whole. One vowel, found in many languages, stands out from this generalization, and that is the mid-central vowel 'schwa' [ə], as at the end of English *sofa*. We will return to this vowel in a later section.

Let's turn now to consonant systems. Comparing the space of possible vowels with that of possible consonants is like comparing navigation at sea with navigation on land. On the open sea there are no landmarks, and motion in any direction is possible. On land there are easy routes and obstructions and the set of possible movements is more peculiarly channelled. The basic space of vowels can be modelled in terms of smoothly continuous dimensions along which there are no privileged points in the middle. The acoustic/articulatory space of possible consonants is more complex and lumpily structured than the vowel space. The 'consonantal landscape' has salient points along the vocal tract where controlled narrowings are more feasible than at others, with complex acoustic effects. Added to this is the fact that, for consonants, air may be moved through the vocal tract by mechanisms that are never used for vowels. There are 'implosives', in which the air is briefly sucked into the mouth, and 'ejectives', which use the tightly closed larynx (as in a glottal stop) as a piston to push air up through the mouth—not to mention click consonants, where the inward movement of air is initiated and contained entirely within the mouth (so you can breathe in or out continuously through your nose while making repeated click sounds). Thus, a weighty challenge to the next generation of language evolution researchers would be to do the same for the consonant systems of the world's languages as de Boer has done for the vowel systems. It hasn't been done yet.

Nevertheless, it is clear that the same competing pressures of distinctiveness and ease of articulation play the most significant role in shaping the consonant systems of languages. Phoneticians Björn Lindblom and Ian Maddieson crisply summarize the situation: 'Consonant inventories tend to evolve so as to achieve maximal perceptual distinctiveness at minimum articulatory cost'—just like vowels, naturally enough, as we have seen. Ease of articulation plays a greater role in the selection of consonant systems than in the selection of vowel systems. In particular, consonants with the implosive, ejective, and click air stream mechanisms mentioned above are all more difficult to make, and rarer in languages. Even for less 'exotic' sounds, there are apparent differences in the ease with which they may be controlled, so that, for example, voiced fricatives are a bit 'harder' than voiceless fricatives. A survey of facts such as these led Maddieson and Lindblom to posit a three-level hierarchy of consonants, labelled 'basic', 'elaborated', and 'complex'. Across languages, the basic consonants are as follows:

[p] as in English *pip*	[tʃ] as in English *church*
[t] as in English *tit*	[m] as in English *Mum*
[k] as in English *kick*	[n] as in English *nun*
[ʔ], glottal stop, as in Cockney *butter*	[ŋ] as at the end of English *sing*
[b] as in English *bib*	[l] as in English *lull*
[d] as in English *did*	[r] as in English *roar*
[g] as in English *gig*	[w] as in English *why* (in most accents)
[f] as in English *faff*	[h] as in English *Hi*
[s] as in English *sis*	[j] as in English *you*

All these basic sounds are found in English, and most of them can occur at both the beginnings and ends of words. Of course, English has other sounds, such as its voiced fricatives [ð] (as in *the*), [v, z], and [ʒ] (as in *rouge*), which are not basic in this sense. The simple Hawaiian consonant system, mentioned earlier, draws exclusively from this basic set.

Other sounds from the IPA chart that beginning phonetics students stretch their vocal tracts around are found in fewer languages. These include, for example: the pharyngeal sounds of Arabic, which require a tense narrowing of the upper throat; retroflex sounds made with the tip of the tongue curled backwards, as in Hindi; lateral fricatives as in Welsh *Llanelli* and *Llangollen*; implosives, requiring a subtle balance between intake of air pulled by a downward moving larynx and quick subsequent resumption of normal outbreath propelled by the lungs; and ejectives, in which the vocal cords are briefly clamped shut and the larynx forced upward to push air outward, accompanied by some plosive or fricative articulation in the mouth. All these and more must be described in a full account of all languages. But due to the relative difficulty in production they are not among the first rank of sounds that languages settle upon. One would not surmise that the earliest languages used such 'exotic' sounds, but rather that they drew from the list of basic consonants above.

One possible exception to the theory that the earliest languages used only a small inventory of basic consonants found widely in all modern languages involves click sounds. What these sounds have in common is the way air is moved, not by any involvement of the lungs, but by sealing off the back of the mouth with the raised back of the tongue, forming some closure further forward in the mouth as for a (click version of) [t] or [p], and drawing air in by pulling the tongue body or jaw downward. So, as a party trick one can make repeated clicks for several minutes while simultaneously breathing in and out. Click sounds are independent of the lungs. In isolation, these sounds are not difficult to make, and some clicks occur as interjections in English, e.g. the tongue-tip click sound sometimes spelt as 'tut-tut'. In the Khoisan languages of southern Africa, there is a wide range of clicks, articulated at different places in the mouth, and sometimes with other action such as voiced lung air going out through the nose. In these languages, the clicks are fully integrated into their sound systems, used distinctively as consonant phonemes. Clicks are indeed typologically unusual, found mainly in Khoisan languages spoken round the Kalahari desert, and in a few other parts of southern Africa, as far away as Tanzania, and nowhere else in the world. The geographical restriction of clicks to the part of the world where the human species originated has led to the suggestion that clicks are archaic remnants of the sound systems of the earliest languages. This suggestion is controversial.

The populations in click-speaking areas are genetically distinct from the surrounding African populations in several ways, having characteristic markers not found elsewhere. This genetic evidence points to a very early separation of the ancestors of modern Khoisan people from the other humans in Africa, at least 100,000 years ago. But there is as yet no evidence of any relevant anatomical or physiological traits characteristic of these populations. Certainly, producing and distinguishing a range of clicks is well within the capability of people from any part of the world. Beginning phonetics students manage it with some effort, without the advantage of Khoisan speakers of being immersed in a click language from birth. Historical linguists raise the objection that languages change their sound systems so frequently that it is unlikely that any class of sounds, clicks or not, could have survived unscathed for 150,000 years. And it is pointed out that clicks have been imported relatively recently into some languages. Furthermore, apart from their having clicks as a common feature, the so-called 'click languages' actually belong to several different language families. This undermines speculation that modern click languages represent some very ancient vestige of the earliest languages. Nevertheless the coincidence of these unusual sounds with the geographical cradle of *Homo sapiens* is intriguing. The debate continues.

Why do some languages evolve out of the comfortable envelope of basic consonants and start to use elaborated and even complex articulations? Perhaps with only a small inventory of basic consonant phonemes not enough semantic distinctions can be made without resorting to longer words or circumlocutions. Perhaps more unusual sounds begin to carry a certain social status, marking off one tribe from another. We don't know why it happened. We do know that when languages spoken by small numbers slowly die, due to dwindling populations and overwhelming contact with major languages, such unusual sounds are the first to disappear. In late stages in the death of a language, such sounds are even rarer than across the board in languages as a whole. When words with such complex sounds are borrowed into other languages, these sounds are often simplified to more basic sounds. And these elaborated and complex consonants are also usually acquired late by children, in any language.

The next consonants and a new vowel

The 'basic' list of consonants from the previous section is arguably still too large, including some sounds that were probably not among the first to be used by the earliest languages. The evidence is from known typical paths of change in languages, which tend to go in one direction only. Short cuts taken to minimize effort in speaking can become conventional, and in this way sounds can appear in languages which are not originally chosen for their maximal distinctness from other sounds. Among consonants, [h] and [ʔ] (glottal stop) and many fricatives are such sounds. In the histories of modern languages using these sounds, there is a one-way process leading to them.

Take [h] first as an example. English [h], as in *hen, horn*, and *hundred*, is historically derived, via Germanic, from an Indo-European [k] sound. Such a sound change is not uncommon in languages. It involves a lessening of the articulatory detail in the sound. For [k], the back of the tongue has to be humped up and back to touch the soft palate. For [h] no such careful placement of the tongue is necessary; it just needs to be out of the way and ready for the next sound. This weakening, or lessening of articulatory distinctiveness, happens often in the histories of languages, but the reverse process is very rare, if it happens at all. (Note now that English [h] itself has undergone the ultimate weakening in some dialects, by disappearing altogether. 'enry 'iggins in Bernard Shaw's *Pygmalion* (better known through the musical *My Fair Lady*) struggled to get Eliza not to drop 'er haitches, as her native Cockney accent allowed.) Another case of a language weakening a sound to an [h] and finally letting it disappear is seen in Spanish. The Spanish verbs *hablar* 'speak' and *hacer* 'do' are derived from Latin *fabulare* and *facere*, along with many other derivations illustrating this sound change. Around the tenth century, these Spanish words were still pronounced with an audible [h], but this is now lost, or 'silent'. Again, the detailed information of lip–teeth articulation in an [f] sound was eliminated, preserving only the voiceless continuant character of [h]. The only way [h] appears in languages is through a process of weakening from other more distinctive sounds (or through borrowing words with [h] from other languages). Thus the very earliest languages probably didn't have [h] in their phoneme inventories, though they may very quickly have adapted to use this sound. A language needs to have at least a little bit of a history to have an [h] sound.

The glottal stop sound, [ʔ], is like [h] in not involving any detailed articulation in the mouth, just a brief clamping together of the vocal cords. This sound also is at the end of a one-way process of historical change. In Arabic, an original voiceless uvular plosive, pronounced with the back of the tongue humped up backward to touch the uvula, has become weakened to [ʔ] in Cairo Egyptian, one of the major colloquial Arabic dialects. In some English dialects, such as Cockney and Glaswegian, [ʔ] replaces [t] after a vowel, as in *got* and *better*. Here again, the detailed articulation of a sound has been lost. Like [h], glottal stop is a sound that only develops as a phoneme in a language through weakening of other more distinctive sounds. The glottal stop is unlikely to have been a sound used by the very earliest languages, though the historical processes of weakening might have begun to set in very early, resulting in a language soon getting a glottal stop in its consonant inventory.

I'll move briefly now to fricatives, with an emphasis on voiced fricatives in particular. Fricatives are sounds in which air passes through a narrow constriction made in the mouth, with a rushing noise. The sibilant [s] is a good example of a fricative, made by the tongue tip approaching, but not touching, the roof of the mouth just behind the teeth. [s] is a voiceless fricative, made with no concomitant vibration of the vocal cords. Its voiced partner is [z]. Other fricative pairs are [f] and [v], [ʃ] and [ʒ] as in *pressure* and *pleasure* respectively, and [θ] and [ð], as in *ether* and *either* respectively. [x] the sound at the end of Scottish *loch* or German *Ach* is a voiceless fricative. In the history of languages generally, a widespread process known as 'lenition', literally 'softening', takes place. By lenition, voiceless plosives such as [p, t, k] can become voiceless fricatives such as [f, s, x]. The famous group of sound changes in the history of Germanic languages known as Grimm's Law includes just such processes, exemplified by such Latin/English correspondences as *pater/father* (p → f), *tres/three* (t → θ), and *canis/hound* (k → x → h). (English words are not, of course, directly derived from Latin, but Latin preserved the original Indo-European sounds in these cases.) The [s] in Standard German *es* and *das* is a lenition of an earlier [t], still preserved in Dutch as *het* and *dat*, in Berlin vernacular as *et* and *dat*, and English *it* and *that*. We see lenition of voiceless plosives also in broad Liverpool (Liverpudlian) English, where words such as *hit* and *lock* end with voiceless fricatives, sounding more (but not exactly) like Standard English *hiss* and Scottish *loch*.

In a further stage of lenition, voiceless fricatives, e.g. [f, s], can become voiced, e.g. to [v, z]. Examples of the former can be seen in German/English alternations such as *Ofen/oven* and *Schaufel/shovel.* Inside English itself, some related pairs of words show lenition of a voiceless fricative to a voiced one, as in *hoof/hooves, knife/knives, half/halve, glass/glaze, loose/lose, breath/breathe.* Here the plurals and verbs once had a second syllable with a vowel, so the consonant in question was between two vowels, a prime site for this kind of lenition. Another historical source of voiced fricatives, also by a kind of lenition, is from voiced plosives. Compare English *over, have, love,* and *raven,* all with [v], with German *über, haben, Liebe,* and *Rabe,* which preserve a more ancient [b]. Similarly the initial dental voiced fricative, [ð], in English *this, that, the, father,* and *mother* comes from an earlier [d]. In the case of *mother* and *father,* this [d] itself had been lenited from an earlier [t], so there were intermediate forms sounding like *mudder* and *fader.*

In sum, several well-trodden paths of historical sound change, versions of lenition, lead to voiced fricatives. Far fewer paths lead back away from voiced fricatives to 'stronger' sounds. Lenition is common, and fortition, an opposite process, from weak sounds to stronger sounds, is much rarer. Notice that in Maddieson and Lindblom's list of basic consonants there are only two fricatives, [f] and [s], both voiceless; there are no voiced fricatives in the list. Further, the distribution of fricatives in the world's languages is somewhat skewed, as Australian aboriginal languages (on about 200 of which there is data, even though some are now extinct) have (or had when they were alive) no fricatives. It comes as a shock to realize that such apparently simple sounds as fricatives could be entirely lacking in a large language family. Extrapolating from all this, it is reasonable to speculate that the very earliest languages, as yet without a history of sound change behind them, would have had no voiced fricative sounds, and maybe even no fricatives at all.

Finally, there is one vowel, now quite common in the languages of the world, that is also unlikely to have been in the inventories of earliest languages. This is the 'schwa' vowel, [ə], as in the second syllable of English *sofa.* This vowel is not near the edge of the articulatory/auditory vowel space, but right in the centre. Schwa, [ə], is typically unstressed and alternates with stressed vowels in related words. Compare, for example, the English words *economy* and *economical*, in which different syllables are stressed. In *economy* [ɪkɒnəmɪ], the second vowel is stressed, and the third vowel is the unstressed schwa. In *economical* [ɪkə'nɒmɪkəl], the situation is reversed, with the second vowel as unstressed schwa. Clearly these words are in systematic alternation. Rather than contrasting with stressed [ɒ], the schwa vowel is a variant of it in which contrast is suspended. In English, schwa is the classic weak vowel, not used in any crucial contrasting function, but as a variant of (almost) any vowel in unstressed position. The factors that give rise to a schwa vowel are thus different from the pressure for distinctiveness described in the previous section. Not all languages have a schwa vowel, weakening an unstressed vowel as English does. But many languages with similar rhythmic properties to English have an equivalent to the English schwa vowel. It seems likely that the earliest languages, before they had had time to evolve such weakening rules, would not have had a schwa vowel.

People make things messier

So far, this is a story of how orderly pronunciation evolves from inarticulateness. The sounds that I have blithely mentioned as emerging in vowel and consonant systems are 'phonemes' in any of the languages in which they have been noted. That is to say that if, for example, [p] is said to be available as a speech sound, then a sound with the broad characteristics of a voiceless bilabial plosive is used systematically in some language somewhere to distinguish words. Arabic, for instance does not make a phonemic distinction between [p] and [b], so that if you were to mispronounce Arabic *baab* 'door' as [paap], it might be considered odd, but you wouldn't be taken as uttering a different word. But a distinction between [p] and its near phonetic neighbour [b] is common in other languages, and so [p] gets listed as one of the basic consonants available to humans, as we have seen. This presupposes that for each language a tidy list of its phonemes can be drawn up.

But all is not so simple. Different languages have slightly different versions of the sounds I have mentioned, and languages systematically modify them in the stream of speech. The modification effects in particular have a significant role in forming the phonological systems that languages end up having. But first I'll briefly mention the ways in which different languages may interpret the 'same' basic consonants and vowels. With vowels, it is particularly easy to see. Even between different speakers of what would count as the same dialect of a language, the vowel in a given word can be regularly different. If I say *man*, for example, its acoustic properties vary from one use to the next, and the range of these uses is different from the range of uses in my friend's pronunciation of the 'same' vowel, even though most people would say we have the same accent. So the alleged [a] sound is not a constant thing, but a rough target area in the vowel space. And between languages, say Standard British English and Standard German, one would use the same phonetic symbol, [a], for the vowel in English *man* as for the vowel in German *Mann*, though they are clearly a bit different. Likewise for consonants. Some English speakers have a version of [t] in which the tongue tip is held slightly closer to the teeth than it is for other English speakers, for example. Nevertheless it is useful to lump all these slight variants under the general heading of [t]. Across languages there is more variation, but we can still usefully identify particular common target ranges of consonants. The [t] in Dutch is less aspirated than that in English, for example, but they are both, for the purposes of listing the solutions that languages settle upon, versions of [t]. In both languages, something with the broad characteristics of a [t], namely a voiceless alveolar plosive, carries meaningful distinctions when contrasted with near phonetic neighbours, such as [d].

Speakers want to get our messages across clearly, and so are somewhat careful not to blur the distinction between one word and another. If we mean *pet* we don't say *pat*, mostly. But studies of words in use show that the variants of phonemes in speech do in fact overlap with each other, giving rise to potential confusion. Confusion is normally avoided because there is enough other information in the signal to allow a hearer to infer what was probably intended. If I seem to be talking about 'my pat dog', you make allowances and quickly understand that I'm talking about my pet dog. Some sloppiness in speech is universal in languages, motivated by minimization of effort, and is universally adjusted to by hearers.

The mouth parts are constantly on the move in speech, and speakers anticipate the upcoming sounds and take short cuts to reach them. Sounds influence their neighbouring sounds. Remarkably, the most convincing mechanical speech synthesis systems don't actually deal in 'sounds', i.e. phonetic segments, at all, but rather in so-called 'diphones', which are the transitions between segments. As a simplified example, the word *bad* would be stored in the computer as consisting, not of three phonemes, but of four diphones, namely the transitions silence-to-/b/, /b/-to-/a/, /a/-to-/d/, and /d/-to-silence. Roughly speaking, each diphone is the second half of one sound followed by the first half of the next. This multiplies the number of entities the machine has to store, but that is no problem, and the results in synthesized speech are often indistinguishable from a real human voice.

The modification of sounds by their neighbours, motivated by haste to get a message across and physical inertia in the mouth-parts, leads to partial breakdown of systems of contrast among sounds. Often it doesn't matter, because a message is clear enough from its context. The neutralization of some contrasts can become conventionalized in the histories of languages. As a result, it is characteristic of phonological systems that they show alternations between sounds in some phonetic positions that in other positions would carry a meaningful distinction. In English, one has to say that [s] and [z] are distinct phonemes, because they keep *Sue* and *zoo*, and *bus* and *buzz*, separate, among many examples. But the plural suffix spelt -*s* can be pronounced with either [s] or [z], as in *cats* [kats] or *dogs* [dɒgz], depending on the kind of sound, voiced or voiceless, that precedes it, and no difference in meaning is conveyed. Likewise, the English past tense suffix, spelt -*ed*, is variously pronounced with a [t] as in *backed*, [bakt], or a [d] as in *lived* [lɪvd], despite the fact that in other positions it really matters whether you say a [t] as in *tie* or a [d] as in *die*. These departures from a rigorous application of 'phonemehood' are a historical consequence of people over the generations taking economical shortcuts with their pronunciation. Neutralization of contrast can never go too far, or communication would be badly affected. Communities strike a balance between ease of pronunciation and getting a message across, with the result that we see alternations in modern phonological systems that do not uniformly respect contrasts in all positions in a word.

The German phonological system makes extensive use of 'Umlauting'—changing the pronunciation of a vowel from a back tongue position to a front tongue position. Examples are *Rad/Räder* [rat/redər] 'wheel/wheels'; *Buch/Bücher* [bux/byçər] 'book/books'; *Loch/Löcher*, [lɔx/lœçər] 'hole/holes'. Such alternations, now firmly fixed in the pronunciation system of the language, are the historical outcome of sound changes in the quite remote past, motivated by ease of articulation, becoming conventionalized. In the examples just cited, the phonetic neighbours which originally prompted these alternations have themselves been elided out of the language, so that the productive Umlauting process can only be fully explained in terms of how the language once was, not as it is now. It is another example of something in language only making sense in the light of evolution, in this case cultural evolution of a sound system descending with modification across many generations.

Further reading

Scientific articles giving more details of the facts and theories sketched here are easy to find with a search engine and a canny choice of keywords. Many, unfortunately, cost money, unless you have access through a university licence; but informative abstracts of articles are typically free. A very useful regular and up-to-date service on recent developments in language evolution is provided by Martin Edwardes at his website named Evolutionary Anthropology Online Research Cluster (EAORC), at http://martinedwardes.webplus.net/eaorc.html. Books on this subject are not so easily located via search engines, and I list some of the major recent overview books below. They are academic in tone, but have much that is accessible to an interested non-specialist.

Christiansen, M. and S. Kirby (eds) (2003). *Language Evolution*. Oxford: Oxford University Press.

Fitch, W. T. (2010). *The Evolution of Language*. Cambridge: Cambridge University Press.

Hurford, J. R. (2007). *The Origins of Meaning*. Oxford: Oxford University Press.

Hurford, J. R. (2011). *The Origins of Grammar*. Oxford: Oxford University Press.

Johansson, S. (2005). *Origins of Language: Constraints on Hypotheses*. Amsterdam: John Benjamins.

Tallerman, M., and K. R. Gibson (eds) (2012). *The Oxford Handbook of Language Evolution*. Oxford: Oxford University Press.

Derek Bickerton has written many books on language evolution. His most recent, less technical, and very readable, books are:

(2008) *Bastard Tongues*. New York: Hill & Wang.

(2009) *Adam's Tongue*. New York: Hill & Wang.

The book series *Oxford Studies in the Evolution of Language* has about thirty books on aspects of language evolution.

Index

Printed and bound by CPI Group (UK) Ltd, Croydon, CR0 4YY